ARUN CHAKRAVORTY '16, a computational biology and computer science major in the College of Arts and Sciences, with his dad, Kishore, his mom, Sumita, and his brother Anshuman. Arun is from San Jose, California.

W9-AXU-704

ALAN NYIRI

JOHN CLEESE, a visiting professor at Cornell

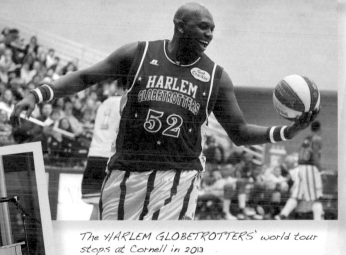

The HARLEM GLOBETROTTERS' world tour stops at Cornell in 2013

RACHEL YAN '14, a student in the College of Agriculture and Life Sciences.

JANE GOODALL often talks at Cornell

Spirited song at Reunion 2012

MADELINE KIEP '16, a student in the College of Arts and Sciences, with her parents Sigrid and Robert Kiep. Madeline is from Haddonfield, New Jersey.

JULIA GUACELLI '16, a student in the School of Hotel Administration, with her brother, André, her dad, Flavio, and her mom, Katia. Julia's hometown is Short Hills, New Jersey.

© Cornell University 2013. Requests for permission for use should be directed to: Dean of Students, Cornell University.

Produced by Cornell University Communications:
Editing: Katelyn Godoy
Design: Wendy Kenigsberg
Photography: Robert Barker, Lindsay Madsen France, Jason Koski
    Photography Archives: Corey Chimko
    Photography Post Production: Matthew Fondeur
    Photography Scheduling: Anitra Whitt
All photography by Cornell University Photography unless otherwise noted

08/13 VIL 8.5M

Cornell University has an enduring commitment to support equality of education and employment opportunity by affirming the value of diversity and by promoting an environment free from discrimination.

Association with Cornell, either as a student, faculty, or staff member, involves participation in a free community where all people are recognized and rewarded on the basis of individual performance rather than personal convictions, appearance, preferences (including sexual or affectional orientation), or happenstance of birth.

Cornell University's history of diversity and inclusion encourages all students, faculty, and staff to support a diverse and inclusive university in which to work, study, teach, research, and serve.

No person shall be denied admission to any educational program or activity or be denied employment on the basis of any legally prohibited discrimination involving, but not limited to, such factors as race, color, creed, religion, national or ethnic origin, sex, sexual orientation, gender identity or expression, age, disability, or veteran status. Cornell University is an affirmative action/equal opportunity employer.

Concerns and complaints related to equal opportunity in education and in employment based on aspects of diversity protected under federal, state, and local law, including sexual harassment complaints filed by any member of the Cornell community against an academic or nonacademic staff member, as well as complaints arising under Title IX should be directed to Workforce Policy and Labor Relations, 391 Pine Tree Road, Ithaca, N.Y. 14850; 255-4652; equalopportunity@cornell.edu.

Cornell University is committed to assisting those persons with disabilities who have special needs related to their educational pursuit or employment. Information on services provided to prospective and current Cornell students with disabilities can be obtained by contacting the Student Disability Services Office, 420 Computing and Communications Center, Ithaca, New York 14853-2081, (607) 254-4545. Prospective employees in need of a workplace accommodation pursuant to the Americans with Disabilities Act or New York state law should contact Workforce Policy and Labor Relations, 391 Pine Tree Road, Ithaca, NY 14850; 254-7232; equalopportunity@cornell.edu. Current employees in need of a workplace accommodation pursuant to the Americans with Disabilities Act or New York state law should be directed to Medical Leaves Administration, 365 Pine Tree Road, Ithaca, NY 14850, (607) 255-1216; email jrd14@cornell.edu.

ON THE COVER:
OreOluwa Badaki '12, College of Agriculture and Life Sciences;
majors: development sociology and inequality studies

Voices

Stories of insight and experience

Cornell University
2013

TABLE OF CONTENTS

"The spirit of
intellectual
exploration
and passion
for learning
are the core
of the
first-year
experience."

—Carol Grumbach '78, JD '87

Welcome to Cornell University

David J. Skorton, president

Dear Cornell families,

Welcome to Cornell University, and congratulations! We are so proud to have you join our community. Many of you are probably feeling some of the pride and elation, as well as a touch of nervousness, that I remember feeling several years ago when my son went off to college. This book can help you understand the university and your student's experience here, and I hope you will keep it close at hand and consult it as that experience develops. Here you will find practical information about Cornell as well as insights from students, faculty, and staff, many of them with expertise in areas about which you may have questions, such as academics, residence life, student health, social norms and behavior, and more.

I am deeply proud of Cornell University, and before I say more about your student's experience here, let me tell you why. In 2015, Cornell will reach its 150th birthday. It was founded with the intention—rare in those days—that it would serve men and women of any race or ethnicity, and that it would not only offer the classical subjects, today usually called the "liberal arts," but also practical studies that would advance agriculture and industry. Encapsulated in

David Skorton and Robin Davisson

Ezra Cornell's words, "I would found an institution where any person can find instruction in any study," that commitment to wide-open opportunity and public engagement remains embedded in Cornell's character today.

As the land-grant university of New York State, Cornell shares knowledge and resources that improve life in communities close to home and around the world. It welcomes students of all backgrounds from across the United States and from 119 other countries. As the first in my family to graduate from college, I know how important it is for a university to offer affordable access and support students through the challenges they will face once enrolled. In this book you can learn more about Cornell's comprehensive health services, programs to encourage healthy living, recreational opportunities, and sources for academic help and support.

This book will also help you think about your role in your student's life. Although your student is, in many ways, an independent young adult, you—parents and other family members and friends—are still essential during these crucial years. How can you best support your student's well-being and success? When is it wise to let your student find ways to cope with challenges, and when—and how—should you assist? Here you'll find insights from people who have worked with thousands of undergraduates and who, every day, carry out Cornell's deep commitment to promoting student health and well-being while providing a world-class education.

Like you, I want your student to make the most of these college years, to learn and grow and take advantage of all that Cornell offers, and to thrive. I hope you find this collection helpful as you support your student's journey. Again, welcome!

Welcome to the Cornell Family

Susan H. Murphy '73, PhD '94, vice president, Division of Student and Academic Services, Cornell University

Susan Murphy '73, PhD '94

"We encourage them to get involved in something beyond the classroom so they can develop talents and attributes beyond their intellect . . ."

I am so pleased that you are joining more than 250,000 Cornell alumni, family members, and friends from around the world. We make up an extraordinary network that cares deeply about our university, especially our students. With your student joining us in the fall, you now are part of this connected Cornell community.

I write this message wearing two hats. First, I am the proud stepmother of two Cornellians, so I know very well many of the emotions you now have and the experiences to come. I also serve as the chief student affairs officer for the university. In this role I have the privilege of working closely with many colleagues who will touch your Cornellian's life in the coming years and hopefully will meet your student as well. I would like to share some thoughts with you from both of those perspectives.

Both Sarah and Julia graduated from Cornell . . . one on the four-year plan and the other on the seven-year plan (if you could call it a plan). Sarah's four-year journey was quite a traditional one.

Julia and Sarah with their dad at graduation

She lived on North Campus her first year, joined a sorority and lived there during her sophomore year, lived off campus as an upperclassman, participated in Cornell in Washington as a junior, and, through The Cornell Tradition, had a summer internship in her junior-senior summer that led to a job offer after graduation. She was enrolled in the College of Arts and Sciences, graduating as an American government major, and now works for the federal government—a career she has had almost since she graduated. While at Cornell she played in the orchestra, dated an ROTC cadet, and by all measure embraced the university completely. She would tell you that her happiest grade was a D+ in calculus her first year, because that meant she did not have to repeat the course. (Her overall GPA, by the way, was much, much higher than this, fueled in large part by her very strong performance during her Cornell in Washington experience and beyond.)

Her sister went to a very different Cornell. Julia did not live on North Campus as a first-year student. After a difficult first semester, she dropped out to live in Ithaca for a while and then to follow the Grateful Dead for two years. Eventually, she returned to school; first to a community college where she aced her work, then to Cornell in summer school where she

Left: Dragon Day celebration 2012

also excelled. To her dad's and my delight, she decided to return to Cornell to complete her degree, but she wanted to change courses of study from human development (in the College of Human Ecology) to creative writing (in the College of Arts and Sciences). So, in the year she was going through the internal transfer she lived at home (quite the change from following the Dead!) because she wanted to focus on her grades to facilitate the transfer. Once accepted into creative writing, she moved to a co-op, where she lived with undergraduates and graduates, and then finished her senior year living off campus. While at Cornell, Julia participated in little beyond the classroom experience except for her commitment to the co-op and her dear friends. The first time she was in Schoellkopf Stadium was for her graduation. She, too, is wonderfully employed and is using her writing talent every day, albeit in a very different form than her poetry composition.

By the way, they both are wonderful moms to my three precious grandchildren.

I share this personal anecdote because I want to underscore the reality that each student who goes through Cornell does so in his or her own way . . . and there is no right or wrong path, really. If I did not understand this fact from my daughters, it is reinforced every day when I meet students. Each one is ready to embrace all that this university has to offer at his or her own pace. Some start as soon as they arrive in August of the first year; others take more time. Regardless of the pace or the direction, each Cornellian eventually finds his or her way, and my colleagues on the staff and the faculty, and our student staff, are here to support, guide, perhaps challenge, and eventually applaud the student's work.

Susan Murphy in 1973, during her senior year at Cornell

Cornell is rich with opportunities—sometimes so rich it can be overwhelming to students. We tell our students, "If you learn anything while you are here, learn to ask for help," and then we give them a help sheet that is four pages long! For the confused new student, this can be too much information; for the savvy senior, it is a great compilation of the many places they can turn. We encourage them to get involved in something beyond the classroom so they can develop talents and attributes beyond their intellect, and then we tell them we have nearly 1,000 organizations from which to choose! What I hope is that together we can help guide your Cornellian through the many options and avenues so he or she can ultimately determine a path that complements his or her unique skills and interests.

Note that I used the word "guide." As family members, you will be among the first to whom your student will turn. After friends and peers, family members are the most trusted source of information. Thus, you will get a phone call or text or instant message with a question well before we do. I encourage you to listen intently but try not to answer the question right away. Rather, help your family member determine the real issue and where the answer might reside. It is so easy today

for students to be in touch with their families; in fact, our research tells us that it is not unusual for many students (especially females) to be in touch daily. This is quite the change from the days when students called home on Sunday afternoons when the rates were low. Such is the advantage of today's technology . . . and the disadvantage. The easy and instant communication can keep us much better connected than ever before, but it can also lead to dependencies that can become unhealthy.

This dependency can happen with high school friends as well as family members. For some of our students, the process of making new friends is daunting. They do not have a consciousness about how they made their best friends at home because they always seemed to be there. Now, those high school friends can still always seem to be there. If your Cornellian is struggling to make a new home, again, listen, sympathize and then guide him or her to some ways to forge new connections. When he or she does, I am confident that life-long friendships of a very special nature will emerge.

One last thought. Encourage your Cornellian to get to know at least one faculty member a semester well enough so that professor can write a letter of recommendation. This piece of advice is one given by my colleague at Harvard, Richard Light, in his book *Making the Most of College*. One might think you need not state the obvious. However, some of our students feel intimidated by the accomplished faculty leading the class and are afraid to approach that person individually. Others simply assume the faculty member would not be interested in making such a connection. Both perceptions are wrong.

The faculty members are not only in the classroom and labs; they also serve as academic advisors, and every undergraduate has one. They live in the residence halls on North Campus and lead the house systems on West Campus. They dine with students and serve as advisors for every athletic team and student organization. Many are engaged in the community with students, and quite a number involve students in their research. They are active members of this community who want to get to know the students beyond the classroom. It always pains me when a student comes to see me as graduation approaches, saying they do not know a faculty member well enough to seek a letter of recommendation. That student has missed a very special part of the Cornell experience.

As you read through this incredible compendium, I trust you will gain an appreciation of the range of opportunities that awaits your Cornellian and the vast array of support that exists. If ever you have a concern, please do not hesitate to be in touch with us so that we can help you help your Cornellian. Should you have the opportunity to visit the campus, I hope you will stop by my office at 311 Day Hall. I would love the chance to meet you in person and to thank you for sharing your family member with us for the coming years.

"Encourage your Cornellian to get to know at least one faculty member a semester well enough so that professor can write a letter of recommendation."

Top (left to right): College of Engineering students Daniel Menendez '08 (left) and Nicole Ceci '08 (right) help steady a PVC pipe that will deliver flocculated water to the bottom of the sedimentation tanks at the Marcala water treatment plant site in Honduras / Johnson Graduate School of Management students give Center for Sustainable Global Enterprise presentations to corporate sponsors / Students in the biomedical engineering lab create an artificial ear using 3D printing and injectable molds / Susan Murphy with Nicholas Booker-Tandy, an applied economics and management major in the College of Agriculture and Life Sciences, with a focus in marketing

Joining Your Student's Journey

Kent L. Hubbell '67, the Robert W. and Elizabeth C. Staley Dean of Students, Cornell University; professor, Department of Architecture, College of Architecture, Art, and Planning

Kent Hubbell '67

"We believe that having the chance to study at Cornell is an opportunity of a lifetime, and we look forward to partnering with you in our efforts to make it so for every Cornell student."

Let me extend a warm welcome to you as you embark on what will be an exciting, challenging, and joyous college experience for both you and your student.

This publication is a community effort. It is made up of essays, contributed by faculty, staff, students, and alumni, intended to broadly paint a picture of life at Cornell for the families of our new students. The essays, each with its own voice, are the personal reflections of their authors, introducing the university from their individual perspectives. They offer a bit of advice, a brief presentation of institutional roles, and an appreciation for Cornell's ethos, traditions, and distinction. The articles are accompanied with links, references, and information we trust will prove to be a useful resource now and over the next four years. While mothers and fathers are the ones most directly involved in this undertaking, sisters, brothers, aunts, uncles, and grandparents all take great pride in sending their nieces, grandchildren, or siblings to Cornell; thus, I hope that you will share this volume with other members of your family.

We, the Cornell faculty and staff, care very much about our students. As we teach, mentor, and support them, we come to care about them nearly as much as you do. And while Cornell has traditionally considered its students to be young adults, we increasingly understand how much cognitive and physical development remains to be realized in college-aged students. We also recognize how important you are to the success of your student, so the relationship we look forward to having with you is one of partnership.

My role as Cornell's dean of students is that of principal student advocate. Our 10 departments include an array of programs and services that enrich and support student life beyond the classroom.

We recognize that an undergraduate education is much more than the simple sum of courses and credit hours assembled for a degree. With that in mind, we strive to create a campus environment, both inside and outside the classroom, where students can flourish intellectually, socially, and developmentally.

All of these considerations have prompted us to create this book, which we hope will serve as a resource for you as you navigate Cornell and your evolving relationship with your son or daughter. We believe that having the chance to study at Cornell is an opportunity of a lifetime, and we look forward to partnering with you in our efforts to make it so for every Cornell student. We have sought to make this publication as thoughtful and beautiful as Cornell . . . we hope you agree.

Let me thank all of the faculty, staff, students, and alumni who so generously contributed to this book, as they have strived to illuminate the way for a new generation of students who are joining the Cornell family.

Additionally, special appreciation goes to:

Dee Zajac, dean of students project manager;
Casey Carr, dean of students content consultant; and
Christine Forester, dean of students project coordinator.

Finally, I am eternally grateful to Daniel J. Zubkoff '79 and Pauline Lee '79 for their generous gift that made possible this wonderful collection of articles.

My sincerest thanks to all.

A Letter to New Cornellians

Daniel J. Zubkoff '79, senior partner and member of the executive committee, Cahill Gordon & Reindel LLP
Pauline Lee '79, former advertising executive, current teacher (teaching English to speakers of other languages)

Daniel Zubkoff '79 and Pauline Lee '79

"The picture is filling in. You've had two weeks of classes, and you have favorite places to study—a nook in the architecture library, a couch in the Straight, the stacks in Uris . . ."

So you've arrived. A great deal of anticipation has led up to this moment. And now you're here . . . the settling in starts—dorm room, roommate, organizing drawers and closets, a neatly made bed, finding the dining hall, walking, talking, observing.

Wake up. It's day two. You're really here. People are becoming more familiar. The milieu is less foreign. You start to imagine what is ahead of you. The strangeness is already dissipating. You're ready for this.

Daniel and Pauline at Cornell, circa 1979

The picture is filling in. You've had two weeks of classes, and you have favorite places to study—a nook in the architecture library, a couch in the Straight, the stacks in Uris— places you easily retreat to. You take familiar paths to your destinations. You are establishing routines. You have acquaintances; some are becoming friends. You have dining buddies and people to walk with between classes.

You are starting to externalize and find out what the university has to offer. There are visiting scholars, art exhibitions, theatre performances, club and intramural sports of every kind, movies, and oddball traditions. You're in the game. You belong here.

Pick your classes. Buy your books. Set the alarm. It's time to start.

Immediately it's evident—you have moved up to the next level. Your professors are outlining intellectual journeys that far exceed what you've experienced so far. Your classmates are smart and interesting; there is geographic, economic, and cultural diversity among them. You're in a more complex and captivating social world.

Each day is increasingly comfortable. You notice that your thinking is more textured. You feel yourself formulating novel thoughts and developing new ways of expressing yourself.

And be mindful of important things. Be kind, be considerate, be modest, and be fair. Try to be a better person every day. Be a leader, not a follower. Know that you are creating future memories— make sure they are memories you'll want to have.

Have a great four years!

JAMIE FELTON

Back at the Nest Once They've Flown: What's A Cornell Parent's Role?

David N. DeVries, associate dean, undergraduate education, College of Arts and Sciences

David DeVries

"Beyond the creaturely comforts we provide our children, in those formative years we lay the moral and ethical groundwork for their futures as adults . . ."

I'd like to begin with a line from a poem: "*to labor and not to seek reward*." The great Irish poet, Seamus Heaney, adapts that line from a prayer first uttered by St. Ignatius of Loyola, the founder of the Jesuit Order. Heaney uses the line in his poem "St. Kevin and the Blackbird," which tells the legend of an ancient Irish monk who once, in his narrow monastic cell, stretched his arm out the window only to have a blackbird land in his outstretched palm. The bird nested in the palm, laid her eggs, brooded them, hatched them, fed the newly hatched chicks, guarded them as they fledged, and watched, eventually, as they flew away. All the while the monk kept his arm straight out the window through weeks of Irish weather. As Heaney tells the story, he focuses on Kevin and wonders what he felt through the long stretches of the nesting, brooding, fledging, and eventual flight. According to one reading of that poem, what Heaney describes through the story of Kevin and the bird is the story of being a parent and raising a child. According to that reading of the poem, you have reached the point where the young bird has taken flight and you now have your palm, your hand, and your arm back to yourself. It is time to draw your arm back in the window and turn to the rest of your life.

Still, it is hard to give up the habit of holding your hand out that window and nurturing those fledglings. Now that your fledgling student is a Cornell undergraduate, what is your role? Ideally, you should lean back and watch it happen—watch your daughters and sons and grandsons and granddaughters and nieces and nephews grow through their undergraduate years into the astonishing adults you know they have it in them to become. The question concerning the role parents and families are meant to play in undergraduates' lives is one of perennial interest and was there from the very beginnings of university-style education in the European Middle Ages. It is a question that has been the subject of a great deal of attention more recently in the press, in the academy, even, in fact, in the government (hence the Family Educational Rights and Privacy Act). The topic has developed into a kind of debate between sides we can fairly easily (and perhaps a bit unfairly—most of the writers on this topic are more nuanced than my Manichean dichotomy would suggest) identify as: "butt in" versus "butt out"—a parent should neither be seen nor heard is the essence of the butt out version; parents need to be involved, the butt in.

Most of the essays and books I've read concerning the roles of parents in their college-aged children's lives focus on the children. But what about the parents and families? Once they've fledged and flown, our primary biological purpose is finished. One interesting thing to note: from the medieval beginnings of the university through the nineteenth

Students moving into North Campus residence halls during Move-In Day 2012

Simone Parris '12 (center) in Brooklyn, New York, with her mother, Negia Ross-Parris, and sisters Blossom and Faith

century, the usual age at which sons left home for college was 14. Both the University of Pennsylvania and Cornell, in the 1860s, set the lower age at 14. And, if you think about other adult roles, in medieval and Renaissance Europe, women were often married by the time they were 15. Think of Shakespeare's *The Tempest*. Prospero and Miranda were exiled to the island when Miranda was 3. The play begins 12 years later. By the end of the play, Miranda is betrothed to Ferdinand; she is 15 years old and children aren't far in her future. The gradual extension of dependent adolescence in Western culture, especially in the United States, is a topic of some interest to social scientists and biologists. But it is, or should be, of great interest to all of us. The central argument on the butt out side of the debate about parents' roles in college-children's lives is that the more involved the parent is, the less likely the child is going to be to step out on her or his own as an adult and be ready to shoulder adult responsibilities. We are, as the social scientists like to say, infantilizing our children the more we intrude on their lives.

Terry Castle, in a fascinating essay called, provocatively, "The Case for Breaking Up With Your Parents," argues that the practice of the intrusive parent begins at birth and only accelerates as the years pass. Hence, by the time the child is 17 or 18, late already in the adult formation process by world-historical standards, there are deeply ingrained habits of entanglement. And, of course, as we've all heard, we are now confronted with the bounce back generation: the children who move back into their parents' homes after college and stay and stay . . .

So what to do? Here, I think, are the factors that make things difficult for us. First and foremost is the cost. College costs a great deal of money, and, by paying it, parents feel they have a right to be involved. Almost as problematic is the extreme ease of communication and travel. Even the great distances between some family homes and the campuses on which their children live resolve to a matter of airline flights. We all groan about air travel. But imagine how difficult it would have been to get from Los Angeles to Ithaca in 1868. Of course, all the electronic connections make anywhere seem like home, at least in terms of communication. It is almost too easy to be in touch. Cost is a factor in prompting parental over-involvement. Ease of access is a factor in prompting parental over-involvement. How to address those factors?

"Being a parent is among the most rewarding experiences a human being can have. It is also potentially the most heartbreaking and certainly often the most frustrating."

Of course, everything about being a parent is costly. We don't have children because we want to save money. And, generally, the belief is that we spend well on our children in order to give them advantages that make it more likely they will be successful as they transition into adult life. So, really, if over-involvement in their college lives is detrimental to their development, we are not spending our money wisely. That's a big if, of course, and an if we'll want to discuss.

That still leaves the problem of ease of access. It is a habit, an addiction really. Texting, Facebooking, Skyping—these all are electronic fixes, drugs. If Johnny sends every paper he writes home to have mom and dad tweak it; if every time Jill confronts a choice of what class to take, she texts dad or mom; if Bobby feels the TA or the assistant coach or the assistant dean disrespected him and dad should do something about it . . . where will the line be drawn? Were we really worse off when all we had was a pay phone in the lobby of the dorm and no way in the world to send our papers home to be tweaked, no way in the world to consult with our parents when we were enrolling in classes, no way in the world to complain instantly about things going badly in relationships, and so forth? Again, this is a question for debate.

Being a parent is among the most rewarding experiences a human being can have. It is also potentially the most heartbreaking and is certainly often the most frustrating. When our children are infants and toddlers and pre-schoolers and elementary school students and on up toward high school, our roles as parents are well defined and, in fact, necessary. Little ones can barely feed themselves, clothe themselves, clean themselves, and certainly cannot work out how to earn money for the food, the clothing, the cleaning products. Beyond the creaturely comforts we provide our children, in those formative years we lay the moral and ethical groundwork for their futures as adults; we endow them with habits of mind and behavior that will go a long way toward determining whether they will be successful adults (and I mean success in much more than simply financial success: I mean taking on the responsibilities we all shoulder in our lives as adults). But when they enter that liminal space, that shadow land at the edge of the large world of their adult lives, what are we supposed to do? That window continues to beckon.

PETE HERRON

Parents and Mental Health Matter More Than Ever

Janis Whitlock, research scientist and director, Research Program on Self-Injurious Behavior in Adolescents and Young Adults, Bronfenbrenner Center for Translational Research, College of Human Ecology

Janis Whitlock

"As tempting as it may be to find a way to do more than lend a sympathetic ear, it is in your student's best interest that you do not do more unless you are sincerely concerned for his or her safety."

When most of you left home to attend college or launch your career, connections with family members probably changed radically. For a majority of people over the age of 35 or so, leaving home meant significantly reduced face time, limited phone access, long-distance phone charges, and new friends and opportunities. All of these factors contributed to reduced parental influence. Today's experience of leaving home could not be more different. A 2007 Cornell study found that nearly 30 percent of our undergraduate students, regardless of their year in school, were in touch with their parents by phone daily (often more than once a day) and more than 85 percent spoke to their parents at least once per week (and these numbers do not include texting, Facebook, or other forms of written communication). Moreover, studies find that parents remain a vital source of emotional support, with six of 10 students reporting that they turn to parents for support when sad, anxious, or depressed. In short, despite the distance and growing autonomy that college offers young adults, parents matter.

The large role that contemporary parents continue to play in their college student's life, even sometimes from great distances, comes as a surprise to many of us who did not have such experiences

growing up. Indeed, as someone who studies college mental health and well-being, I had not anticipated that a significant line of my research would involve close examination of the role that parents play in their child's life after he or she has left home. The influential role of parents, however, is evident in more than just their popular nomination as emotional confidants. In several studies of factors that influence the onset or worsening of psychological distress in college students, perceived emotional connection and support from parents consistently emerged as a very powerful element—one that significantly protects students when present, and heightens risk of serious psychological distress when absent.

Discerning between stress and distress

The strong role that parents continue to play creates both opportunities and challenges. Although hearing about your student's day-to-day life can be gratifying and reassuring, it can also leave a parent confused about how to discern between stress and distress—between the normal feelings and experiences that come with being a college student and the unhealthy feelings and perceptions that accompany more serious forms of distress. This is particularly important in light of the fact that late adolescence and early adulthood are the most common times for the onset of mental illness. Both stress and distress are perceived as suffering, and both can feel unmanageable, at least for a while. Stress, however, typically serves

Left: The Baker Tower archway in fall

to motivate action in service of resolution, whereas distress feels chronic and unresolvable to the sufferer. In fact, we know that human beings do not grow or perform well without some stress, so as hard as it can be to regularly hear about your student's stressful events or times, it may help to think of these as growth opportunities. It is important to keep in mind that since college can pose entirely novel experiences for students, they may not feel or seem as resilient as usual—at least at first.

Since the "no news is good news" adage no longer applies in today's college student–parent relationship, it is important to be able to tell the difference between signs and symptoms of healthy, or at least manageable, stress and more serious forms of psychological distress. Here are a few questions you can ask yourself to help figure out how much to worry:

- Is your student's response to whatever is posing challenges consistent with his or her typical response to stress?

- How much are stressful emotions interfering with life (for example, going to classes, socializing, taking care of himself/herself)?

- How long lasting and chronic is your student's negative feeling?

- To what extent is your student repeating the same or worsening negative thoughts and fears?

- Is she or he connecting to people on campus (not just friends from home or other virtual connections)?

- To what extent is he or she taking realistic and productive steps to reduce stress?

Concerning levels of distress bring about chronic feelings of extreme overwhelm that interfere with the ability to function in daily life. While feeling so down that it is hard to get out of bed and function normally can (and does) happen to most of us once in a while, feeling like this for more than a couple of days every now and again is a sign that more help and support may be needed. This, coupled with no local support or connection, does warrant parent intervention.

If you are worried about your student's stability and well-being, please contact the Office of the Dean of Students (607-255-1115) during regular business hours, or call Cornell University Police (607-255-1111) or Gannett Health Services (607-255-5155) any time of day or night.

Helping your student thrive

It is important to possess reasonable and realistic expectations of yourself and your student when he or she leaves for college, particularly in responding to daily stressors. Unlike when your child was living at home, you are not well-positioned to do much more than listen, encourage, and support. As tempting as it may be to find a way to do more than lend a sympathetic ear, it is in your student's best interest that you do not do more unless you are sincerely concerned for his or her safety. Experiencing daily stress, even if it involves feeling really down at times, is a critical part of learning how to productively cope with life, and it offers important opportunities for development and reflection.

Just as leaving for college invites emerging adults to develop new skills and abilities, it invites parents to step fully into new roles as more distal supporters and advisors. Research consistently shows that parental emotional availability is useful in young adult development of autonomy and capacity, but what does this look like? Here are a few tips for offering developmentally useful support and guidance:

- Help your student become aware of his or her own patterns of stress management by asking the questions above and helping him or her to understand the differences between normal and healthy stress and more serious signs of distress.

- Encourage your student to make local connections. Although the Internet offers unparalleled opportunities to stay connected with friends at home, having local friends, confidants, and supporters is imperative for thriving and coping when times are hard.

- Limit your involvement in problem solving to making observations or suggestions. If there are calls to be made, offices to be visited, information to be gathered, or conversations to be had, support your child in taking these steps, but refrain from doing it for him or her, unless it is clearly your jurisdiction.

- Gradually reduce contact to the point that it feels comfortable to go for a week or more without significant exchange. I know this sounds radical for some families; there are a number of students who regard their parent(s) as their best friend(s). And, it need not happen right away. But, it is important that your student have the opportunity to experience herself or himself as capable of going through multiple days without parental check in. Experiencing yourself as capable and resilient is not possible if you do not confront situations that require resilience.

- Model healthy ways of coping. Share your positive strategies for dealing with your own challenges. Your evolution as a parent and a person is a powerful learning opportunity for your student since he or she inevitably identifies with you more than you probably know (or like to think!). Being mindful about how you manage your own stress and sharing that process with your student is even more supportive than simply listening to what is shared because it models authentic growth and development.

Parents are critical allies of the developmental process. Staying connected while supporting separation and the trials and errors that build capacity and confidence is a fine line—particularly in the constant-contact era. There is no right or wrong way of helping children grow; it seems to happen despite us in most cases anyway! When in doubt, reach out for advice and trust that all of us here at Cornell want the best for your child, as well.

ALAN NYIRI

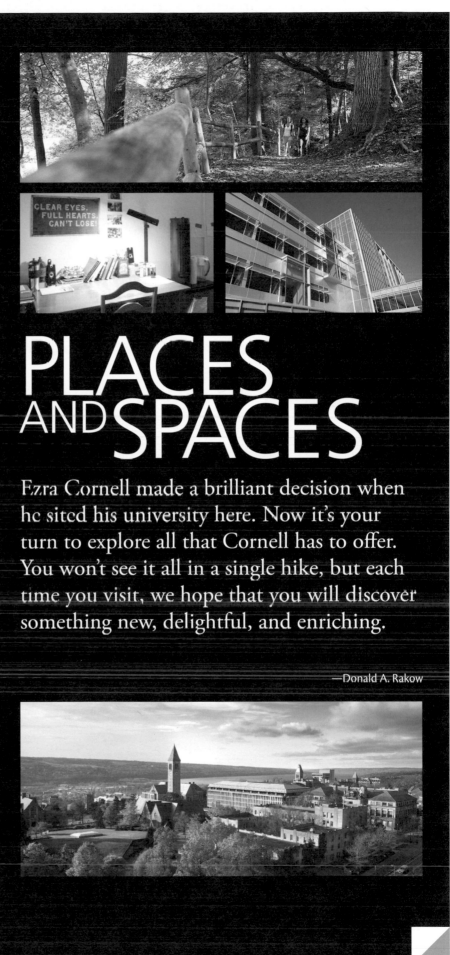

PLACES AND SPACES

Ezra Cornell made a brilliant decision when he sited his university here. Now it's your turn to explore all that Cornell has to offer. You won't see it all in a single hike, but each time you visit, we hope that you will discover something new, delightful, and enriching.

—Donald A. Rakow

The Arts at Cornell University

Kent Kleinman, the Gale and Ira Drukier Dean, College of Architecture, Art, and Planning

Kent Kleinman (right) with Richard Meier '57

"The studio is both place and culture, and for students and faculty in the art disciplines, it is equally house and home."

Art is everywhere at Cornell. Even a cursory survey of Cornell's academic landscape reveals an extraordinary richness of art and design departments, programs, and courses. They are dispersed among multiple colleges and disciplinary fields: the Department of Art, the Department of Performing and Media Arts, the Program in Interior Design, the Department of Architecture, the Department of Landscape Architecture, the Department of Music. The list is long and varied, but there are common characteristics. Most of these programs focus on modes of expression based neither in text nor in symbolic logic, but rather use material, form, and the bodily senses to explore aspects of the human condition. Students in the arts are, in a profound sense, fabricators, in that they craft their work by engaging and reshaping the material world. Art and design students work in particular ways: they work iteratively, responding to their own marks and moves in search of an ever more precise question, for the goal of an artwork is rarely an answer but rather a precise and provocative question. And in contrast to other academic practices, a work of art or design is not submitted and graded. It is exhibited and critiqued, a public event where faculty and students collectively affirm and advance the state of their discipline through discourse and by example.

All this activity requires a specialized environment, a type of space particular to the arts and essential to the education of emerging artists and designers: the studio. The studio is the gravitational core of student life for those in the arts. These are the midnight-oil-burning, drafting-tabled, computer-screened, over-caffeinated centers of art teaching and learning where habits are formed and aesthetic identities are shaped. The work in the studio is open and public, even in embryonic form, so the studio is also a place of trust and collaboration. And anxiety. And debate. In the studio a drawn line can provoke an extended argument; a brushstroke can evoke a historical reference; a sketch can launch a critique of the city; an image can declare a philosophical position. The studio is both place and culture, and for students and faculty in the art disciplines, it is equally house and home. Studios dot the campus. They are easy to spot after sundown.

But learning and teaching in the arts at Cornell is not limited to these specialized academic programs or sites, for there is in fact no clear divide between science and art. In the Department of Fiber Science and Apparel Design, for example, test tubes and sewing machines, artificial skin and skin-clinging fabrics reside side by side, surrounded by hand sketches and MRI scans. In the Faculty of Computing and Information Science, computer scientists and fine art students collaborate on game design, and computer graphic programmers study Vermeer paintings

Left: Olivia Woo, BFA '15: *Wind It (\wind\ or \wīnd\)* (2011), acrylic, 12" x 12" spinnable canvases

in an attempt to capture his light, while art students script programs to insert their art into the digital public realm. Art and design students work with equal facility on printing presses, CNC milling machines, and 3D printers. Scientists in the NanoScale Science and Technology Facility participate in an annual competition for the best photograph captured with an electron microscope, while art students study the etching of silicon wafers in the context of traditional etching techniques.

Then there are the collections: numerous and vast archives that gather together discrete worlds of artifacts into systems of order and classification to facilitate study and reflection. The Herbert F. Johnson Museum of Art is the university's principal venue for exhibitions and events, and it serves classes across campus with its special collections and dedicated study galleries. The Kroch Library Division of Rare and Manuscript Collections is an archive-cum-museum, where the book is revered as much for its text as for its physical presence and material craftsmanship. But perhaps most spectacular is the model collection of invertebrate sea creatures at the Department of Ecology and Evolutionary Biology, comprising more than 540 luminous glass sculptures of sea specimens, hand-crafted by the nineteenth-century glass artists Leopold and Rudolf Blaschka in order to display to scholars and the public those spineless creatures that could not, as it were, be stuffed and mounted.

The web of art on campus is vast. But when I say that art is everywhere at Cornell, I intend more than the sum of the classes, the students, the faculty, the studios, the shops, and the wondrous collections that

support and advance studies in the arts. Quite literally, as a physical place, Cornell itself is a work of art. Much is made of Cornell's natural beauty, of the extraordinary topography and sublime nature. But to experience Cornell is to recognize the remarkable reach of the design arts. To be sure, the natural geology is splendid. But make no mistake: this landscape is designed. It has been crafted carefully and lovingly—indeed artistically—to produce the picturesque quadrangles that define the individual precincts of the arts, agriculture, and engineering colleges. It is tethered audaciously to its surrounding environs with bridges that span two gorges and provide a platform and frame for viewing 400 million years of earthwork below. It has been leveled into terraces and graded into slopes that yield the grand vistas and secluded nooks that generations of Cornellians discover anew each fall semester. Cornell is a collection of very fine architecture, and recently some extremely important works have joined the historic fabric of the campus. But even more than its buildings, Cornell is an ensemble of artfully sculpted open space, carefully trimmed view corridors, measured promenades and meandering pathways, mighty oaks sited decades ago with great care to appear as if they were always thus. All this makes Cornell one of the finest examples of nineteenth-century campus planning in the country; a great, if always unfinished, work of art; and a most fitting canvas for a community of wildly creative students and scholars, regardless of their fields of study.

FOR MORE INFORMATION
College of Architecture, Art, and Planning: aap.cornell.edu

Under the Milstein Hall overhang in spring: the Stiller Arcade, named in honor of Duane '84 and Dalia Stiller, BArch '84

KEN LOEFFLER

"There is in fact no clear divide between science and art."

Top (left to right): Painting studio / Herbert F. Johnson Museum of Art / Utagawa Hiroshige, Japanese 1797–1858, *Suido Bridge at Surugadai,* from the series *One Hundred Famous Views of Edo,* color woodblock print, bequest of William P. Chapman, Jr., Class of 1895, collection of Herbert F. Johnson Museum of Art / Testing a robot in the autonomous systems lab / Erica Sutton '12, College of Architecture, Art, and Planning / Mia Kang '13, graduate student in the College of Architecture, Art, and Planning, in the Schloss drafting studios / Calvin Kim '15, College of Architecture, Art, and Planning, in New York City / Cornell Fashion Collective Runway Show / Kroch Library Division of Rare and Manuscript Collections / *Nowhere and Everywhere at the Same Time* in Rand Hall / The steel sculpture *Universe Cubed* greets visitors to Milstein Gallery during the *LUX Art and Science Exhibition* / Glass sculpture of a sea specimen, hand-crafted by nineteenth-century glass artists Leopold and Rudolf Blaschka / *Unpacking the Nano* exhibit at the Johnson Museum / Leo Villareal's *Cosmos* at the Johnson Museum / A project at the 2012 third-year architecture students' final review reception

Glorious to View

Donald A. Rakow, associate professor, Department of Horticulture; former Elizabeth Newman Wilds Director, Cornell Plantations

Donald Rakow

"Hiking up this gorge trail, one feels embraced by the majesty of nature—and a long way from the rigors of classes."

Cornell is much more than the sum of the classes offered, and more than the buildings that house its classrooms and labs. It is also a unique landscape—forged by glaciers, settled by farmers, and identified by Ezra Cornell as the site on which to build his school of higher learning.

The university's founder envisioned a uniquely open institution "where any person can find instruction in any study." A plainspoken, hardworking son of the land, Cornell was a true democrat, wanting his new university to accept individuals solely on the basis of their qualifications and interests. And the landscape on the hill that had so struck him with its beauty reinforced this sense of democracy, with its varied topography and inspiring views.

The splendor of the Cornell landscape cannot be fully appreciated by a casual drive through campus, especially when its sole purpose is to drop off a daughter or son at a North Campus dorm to begin a life without parents. No, the Cornell experience is one best achieved on foot, because it is only when walking that one can appreciate the true complexity of our land forms.

The central campus is bordered by a pair of deep-cut gorges that were carved after the last ice age. Cascadilla Creek Gorge, which runs along the southern edge of campus, is home to six spectacular waterfalls, diverse plant and animal species, and a 1930s pathway constructed by the Civilian Conservation Corps. Hiking up this third-of-a-mile gorge trail, one feels embraced by the majesty of nature—and a long way from the rigors of classes.

Cascadilla Creek Gorge steps

Looking down from the high rises of North Campus, one spies Beebe Lake, a wide spot in the second gorge corridor, Fall Creek. Beebe Lake was originally a swamp, but was dammed by a young Ezra Cornell to provide year-round power for Colonel Jeremiah Beebe's plaster mill (which Cornell managed at the time). Today, it is a beloved icon to students and alumni, with Sackett Bridge at one end and the powerful Triphammer Falls at the other. After walking around the lake, one can stand on Triphammer Bridge and watch the thundering falls to the east, and to the west see just how deeply the rushing waters have carved the limestone walls that formed the gorge.

After the drama of the two gorges, the central campus may appear flat or tame. But this 786-acre hilltop that Ezra offered to his wife, Mary Ann, as "a garden of Eden for my bird of Paradise" has many more surprises to reveal. Despite the proliferation of new buildings in recent decades, the innate qualities of the landscape remain largely intact. The first set of academic buildings on campus was the "stone row" on the Arts Quad, and just below them, Libe Slope slouches down to West Campus and beyond to the city. A favorite for sledding before it was prohibited, this turf-covered hillside is now the site for Slope Day, a celebration of the academic year's end.

Just southeast of the Slope is the great Gothic student union, Willard Straight Hall, and alongside it in a mini-gorge is the Willard Straight Rock Garden. The unkempt condition of the rock garden lends it a romantic air, a perfect spot for moonlit strolls. The water that runs through the garden is commonly known as Wee Stinky Creek, and uphill from it one finds Wee Stinky Glen. These odd monikers apparently refer back to a time when the College of Veterinary Medicine was located nearby and the creek was used as a drain for chemicals and animal wastes. Fortunately, no odors remain from that less-regulated era.

Up a knoll, near the intersection of Tower Road and East Avenue, sits the A.D. White House, from which Andrew Dickson White, Cornell's first president, could look out the picture windows and see the new campus taking shape before him. The views that White had from that perch are reflective of one of the great qualities of the Cornell landscape—from nearly any point, one gets glimpses of other natural and manmade forms.

Further east, up Tower Road, one arrives at the Agriculture Quadrangle, which is mostly flat. But Mann Library, at its far end, provides views from its glassed rear walls into an old-growth woodland, and the extensively renovated Warren Hall looks down on the Dean's Garden, a horticultural gem. The Dean's Garden is under the management of Cornell Plantations, which operates the botanical garden, wildflower garden, and arboretum that together occupy 200 acres. These are three major components of Cornell's museum of living plants, and each has been developed in a natural depression or bowl.

In many ways, the Plantations' areas are a microcosm of the greater Cornell landscape, with their rolling hills, proximity to water, marvelous view corridors, and surprises around every bend. As the seasons progress, different sections of the Plantations take center stage for their beautiful displays. Early spring is the time to troop over to the Mundy Wildflower Garden, located between Judd Falls Road to the west and Caldwell Road to the east. Within this wooded glen are paths lined with a multitude of native spring ephemerals, from trillium to trout lilies, hepaticas to spring beauties. In summer, many of the collections in the botanical garden—including the Robison Herb Garden, Young Flower Garden, and Pounder Vegetable Garden—offer an abundance of blooms, scents, and textured foliage. Then in fall, the F.R. Newman Arboretum is in its greatest glory, its groves of trees showing off their rich palette of autumnal colors. Even though the plants that fill the Plantations landscape are dormant in winter, this is still a stunning season in which to visit. Nowhere is that more true than in the Mullestein Winter Garden, located in the heart of the botanical garden. Each of the trees and shrubs in the Winter Garden has been selected for its interesting bark, evergreen foliage, colorful berries, or unusual form, so that the overall effect is a visually stunning garden, even though there is not a single plant in bloom.

Ezra Cornell made a brilliant decision when he sited his university here. Now it's your turn to explore all that Cornell has to offer. You won't see it all in a single hike, but each time you visit campus, we hope that you will discover something new, delightful, and enriching.

FOR MORE INFORMATION
Cornell Plantations: cornellplantations.org
Map of the Ithaca campus: cornell.edu/maps
Visiting Cornell: cornell.edu/visiting

Enjoying the fall evening views from the top of Libe Slope

CHRIS KITCHEN

Highlight tour of the Robison York State Herb Garden in the Botanical Garden at Cornell Plantations

A Transformational Campus

Gilbert Delgado, architect, Cornell University; senior director, Capital Projects and Planning

Gilbert Delgado

"And so begins the evolution of the campus:
each epoch is expressed, allowing the observer
to decipher the history of the campus in a way
similar to reading the rings of a redwood tree."

The Cornell University campus begins with a dramatic landscape overlooking Cayuga Lake from more than 800 feet above sea level, separated from the surrounding areas by deep gorges on its northern and southern boundaries. The spectacular view of the lake inspired Frederick Law Olmstead to conceive of a campus plan that included a grand terrace overlooking it. Alas, this idea was never realized—but instead the early buildings were grouped around a magnificent green, forming one of the great American academic public spaces.

For the most part, the earliest buildings were humble structures with ambiguous architectural pedigree, reflecting the practicality of the university's founder, Ezra Cornell. Their rustic stone faces and modest interior spaces were made gracious as they played their part in framing the monumental Arts Quadrangle.

Cornell's first architectural graduate, William Henry Miller, went on to give the university a more delicate treatment in the late nineteenth century, with brick buildings of the Victorian era on the southern end of the Arts Quadrangle. And so begins the evolution of the campus:

Left: Sage Hall, McGraw Tower, and Cayuga Lake at dusk

Sibley Hall before the east and domed center sections were added

each epoch is expressed, allowing the observer to decipher the history of the campus in a way similar to reading the rings of a redwood tree.

In the early twentieth century, a significant building campaign expanded the campus to the east along a level ridge that came to be known as Tower Road. Funded primarily by the state, these buildings were in many ways more consistent than the earlier buildings, which had been endowed by the university. These light-colored brick buildings, serving agricultural and life sciences, were designed

The Physical Sciences Building, designed by architect Richard Meier '57, was awarded LEED (Leadership in Energy and Environmental Design) Gold certification from the U.S. Green Building Council

Milstein Hall, designed by Rem Koolhaas, received LEED Gold certification from the U.S. Green Building Council

in a stripped-down, classical style commonly used for many government buildings of the time. Several years later, the campus extended as the Law School expressed itself in a Collegiate Gothic collection of buildings.

The postwar period brought extraordinary growth to the university. Many would say that some of the buildings built in this era do not move the spirit or contribute to the beauty of the campus. And in some cases, this is undeniable. Fortunately, during the last 30 years, a focus on campus planning and architecture has produced several noteworthy buildings that continue the positive evolution of the campus into the twenty-first century. Five Pritzker Prize–winning architects have designed buildings connecting the university into the larger cultural discussion worldwide. It is fitting that an internationally recognized institution of higher learning be expressed physically by

thoughtful and stimulating architecture based on ideas as innovative as the research conducted within its walls.

It would be impossible to improve on Winston Churchill's famous saying, "We shape our buildings, thereafter they shape us." Students come to Cornell from all over the world. Some come from large cities; some from small towns. In addition to their studies, they will learn about the built environment. The campus and its buildings have the capacity—and the obligation—to teach about the importance of public space, sustainability, craft, beauty, creativity, and all humanistic pursuits that enrich the soul and fashion more complete citizens of the world.

FOR MORE INFORMATION
Cornell Master Plan for the Ithaca Campus: masterplan.cornell.edu

Artist's rendering of the new Alumni Quad, comparable to the Arts Quad in size and intended to be an iconic space for a variety of uses (from Cornell's Master Plan)

MORPHOSIS

Artist's rendering of the new Bill & Melinda Gates Hall

Diversity, Inclusion, and a Place for All

Renee T. Alexander '74, PhD, associate dean of students, Cornell University; director, 6-2-6, Center for Intercultural Dialogue

Renee Alexander '74, PhD

"A truly diverse community is the foundation for the thoughtful and in-depth exchange of ideas."

As a proud member of Cornell's Class of 1974, I bring a unique and important perspective to life on the Hill in this second decade of the twenty-first century.

The old racial paradigm, in which "engaging across difference" was viewed through a black/white lens, has given way to a new generation of young adults who bring their own experiences and ideas, which are impacting campus culture and redefining how students connect with each other. The millennials are pushing boundaries, breaking down barriers, and driving positive change.

Asia Night, the Leadership Roundtable, and Passover Freedom Seder share a common theme: students are engaging across difference and working together to build a cross-cultural campus community.

The future of diversity is now.

A 2013 multifaith Passover Seder

Moving around campus and observing students coming and going makes it remarkably evident that demographic shifts—changes that are reshaping the nation's social fabric and politics—are reflected in our student composition. In many ways, Cornell is a microcosm of the evolving American mainstream, and the class of 2016's profile reflects this reality:

41.3% Caucasian

16.9% Asian American

12.0% Hispanic/Latino

9.2% unknown (not reported)

5.8% Black/African American

2.2% Bi/Multiracial

0.5% Native American/Hawaiian

Habitat for Humanity Truss Days on Ho Plaza

A truly diverse community is the foundation for the thoughtful and in-depth exchange of ideas. It's a place where cross-cultural skills are developed and enacted among diverse campus constituencies, with campus partners, and within the classroom and workplace. And it's an opportunity for everyone to contribute to our intellectual community all that is distinctive and unique about their individual perspectives while expanding horizons, blazing new trails, pursuing new knowledge, and sharing what they have to offer.

Your sons and daughters will experience the rich variations in intellectual approaches, individual backgrounds, cultural nuances, and demographics (race, religion, class, gender, sexual orientation) that make our community a wonderfully diverse place to study, live, and grow. As students settle in and eventually hit their stride, they will have numerous opportunities to embrace the vibrancy, energy, and richness of diverse experiences that are central to a Cornell education.

We support the holistic development of students, both within and beyond the classroom, and to that end, a plethora of resources and supportive services are in place to ensure that all students can maximize their time on the Hill to the best of their ability.

FOR MORE INFORMATION
Cornell Diversity and Inclusion: diversity.cornell.edu

Selamawit Gebre '14 at the 8th Annual Asia Night in Duffield Atrium

6-2-6 Center for Intercultural Dialogue

6-2-6 Center for Intercultural Dialogue (also known as the Intercultural Center) is located at 626 Thurston Avenue on North Campus. The center is home to identity-based programs including the Asian and Asian American Center; Cornell Alumni Student Mentoring Program; Intercultural Programs; Lesbian, Gay, Bisexual, Transgender Resource Center; and Student Development Diversity Initiatives.

A number of student organizations also operate from 6-2-6—the African, Latino, Asian, Native American Intercultural Programming Board; Black Students United; Cornell Asian Pacific Islander Student Union; La Asociación Latina; Leadership Roundtable; [MiX]ed; and Scholars Working Ambitiously to Graduate. Intergroup Dialogue Project, an academic course, also uses the building. While these programs have distinct identities, they all offer collaborative programming that reaches the entire Cornell community and underscores our commitment to break down barriers and work across differences.

The center, open seven days a week, is a hub of activity on North Campus, where meetings, events, dinners, retreats, classes, study groups, and student social activities contribute to a vibrant intercultural atmosphere, where everyone is welcome and friendships are formed.

Stop by and visit while walking our campus—we're adjacent to the Thurston Avenue bridge. Our doors are always open. As a Cornell alumna, I am delighted to welcome your sons and daughters to our community and help them develop intercultural skills that will contribute mightily to a successful career and life.

Welcome to the Cornell family.

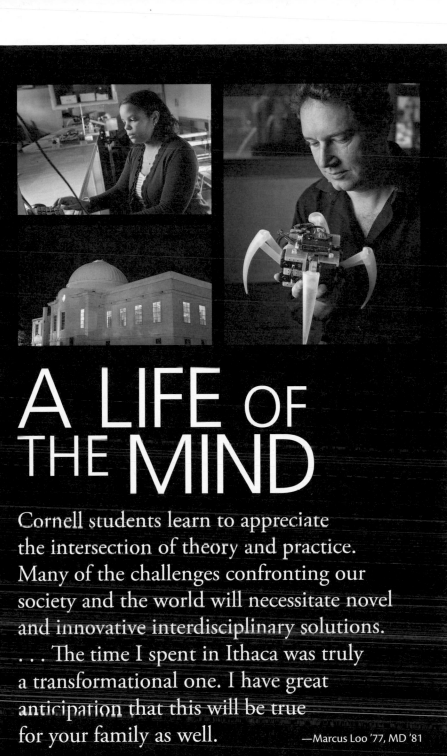

A LIFE OF THE MIND

Cornell students learn to appreciate the intersection of theory and practice. Many of the challenges confronting our society and the world will necessitate novel and innovative interdisciplinary solutions. . . . The time I spent in Ithaca was truly a transformational one. I have great anticipation that this will be true for your family as well.

—Marcus Loo '77, MD '81

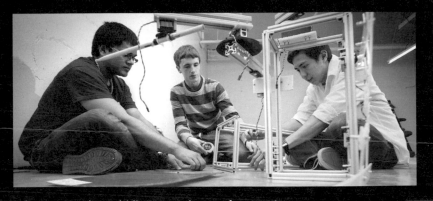

Left: Annetta Alexandridis presses the case for restoring Cornell's collection of plaster casts in Goldwin Smith Hall

150 Years of Tradition and Innovation

Corey Ryan Earle '07, associate director, Student and Young Alumni Programs, Office of Alumni Affairs

In April 2015, Cornell University will reach the sesquicentennial of its founding—its 150th birthday. Although younger than its Ivy League peers, Cornell proudly celebrates a rich history of tradition and innovation as a pioneer in higher education.

Corey Ryan Earle '07

"Cornell isn't just four years; it's forever."

The story of Cornell is one of trail blazing, risk taking, challenges, and setbacks—not unlike the experiences of a first-year Cornell student. It's a tale with relevance to every student who ever snacked on a chicken nugget (invented by Cornell professor Robert C. Baker '43), borrowed a library book (first allowed at Cornell before other colleges), or enjoyed air conditioning (thanks to Cornell engineer Willis H. Carrier, Class of 1901).

I remember my own arrival on campus in 2003, nervous about the swim test and first day of classes. Growing up in the Ithaca area in a family of Cornellians made it easy to take Cornell for granted, but I was captivated as I immersed myself in the campus culture and learned about its past. Every building and plaque represented a story and a Cornellian who changed the world. Now, 10 years later, I "bleed Big Red" as an alumnus, staff member, and lecturer for a 400-student class on Cornell's unique history.

Cornell University was founded in 1865 by two men who wanted to challenge the status quo: Ezra Cornell, a farmer and entrepreneur who believed in the accessibility of education to all, and Andrew Dickson White, a scholar and diplomat who was frustrated by the rote learning and narrow curriculum that characterized most American universities. A national need for practical training in agriculture and engineering led Congress to pass the Morrill Act in 1862, providing support for the establishment of land-grant colleges in each state. This legislation became the catalyst for Cornell and White to join forces and found Cornell University as the land-grant institution of New York State.

Ezra Cornell

Having amassed a fortune in the telegraph business, Ezra Cornell offered a half million dollars and his farm in Ithaca to establish the new university. The plan of organization was drafted by Andrew Dickson White, drawing on his experiences at Yale, Michigan, and prestigious universities throughout Europe. Both men felt strongly about student access for all, freedom from sectarian influences, and the importance of both classical and practical disciplines. The new university would not only have great libraries but also great laboratories and workshops. Their forward-thinking philosophies, combined with the public service mission of the Morrill Act, developed into the foundational principles of the new university.

Left: Archival photos in this essay are part of the Cornell University Library Division of Rare and Manuscript Collections

Dr. James Law, veterinary students, and the famous Auzoux papier mâché horse, circa 1898, which accurately represented 3,000 body parts and could be disassembled into 97 pieces

With White elected as the founding president, Ezra Cornell's stated goal became the university motto: "I would found an institution where any person can find instruction in any study." This radical concept of a diverse student body and broad curriculum placed the new university at the forefront of a national shift in higher education. Cornell was the first major eastern university to admit women as well as men and was among the first nationwide to welcome all students regardless of race or religion at a time when many colleges were presided over by clergy. Cornell broke the mold by offering practical and professional courses of study, like agriculture and engineering, as academic equals to more traditional classical curriculum, like languages, literature, and history. Ezra's school became the model for the modern university and was called the "first American university" by educational historian Frederick Rudolph.

Nearly 150 years later, Cornell remains true to the vision of

its founders and continues to innovate. The four-year programs in architecture, hotel administration, and industrial and labor relations were the first of their kind in the country. A pioneer of electrical engineering

and veterinary medicine in the nineteenth century, Cornell explores new disciplines like nanotechnology, biomedical engineering, and fiber science and apparel design in the twenty-first century. With an eye on the future, plans are underway to build Cornell NYC Tech, an applied sciences campus in New York City.

Cornellians past and present are linked by a sense of history and tradition. We all share a common experience that transcends class year, whether it's passing the swim test, appreciating the natural beauty of campus, parading on Dragon Day, or just hiking up Libe Slope on a snowy winter day. I'm reminded of this Big Red bond each time I see a

Cornell sweatshirt or baseball cap hundreds of miles from Ithaca, usually worn proudly by a parent, alumnus, or alumna.

Being a Cornellian means joining a network that includes more than 250,000

alumni, families, and friends around the world. Their loyalty and enthusiasm (often on display at hockey games) can rival that

of nearly any other university, leading some to call Cornell the "Ivy League school with a Big Ten heart."

Engaged alumni and friends continue to shape Cornell throughout their lives by volunteering their time, talent, and treasure. Cornell isn't just four years; it's forever.

Opportunities abound for current students to interact with alumni, young and old. Alumni mentors can be found via student organizations, career networking events, or as guest speakers on campus. During winter and spring break, regional alumni associations around the world often include students in programming like Cornell Cares Day, an international day of service. Students should proactively seek out these opportunities and take advantage of the alumni network whenever possible. Cornell parents and friends are certainly welcome to participate in the alumni associations and events as well.

Welcome to the Cornell family. You should feel proud to join this legacy. I encourage new students (and families) to learn about and

explore this university that will play a major role in their lives. Cornell's incredible past is unique from that of other institutions of higher learning. When it was founded as a coeducational, nonsectarian university for any person and any study, Cornell changed the face of collegiate education in the United States and in the world. Knowing about and appreciating this home away from home will make time spent here even more rewarding.

FOR MORE INFORMATION
"I Would Found an Institution," The Ezra Cornell Bicentennial
    Exhibition: rmc.library.cornell.edu/ezra
Cornell Traditions: cornell.edu/studentlife/traditions.cfm
Cornell: Glorious to View (Chapter 1) by Carol Kammen:
    ecommons.library.cornell.edu/handle/1813/3091
Cornell University Alumni: alumni.cornell.edu

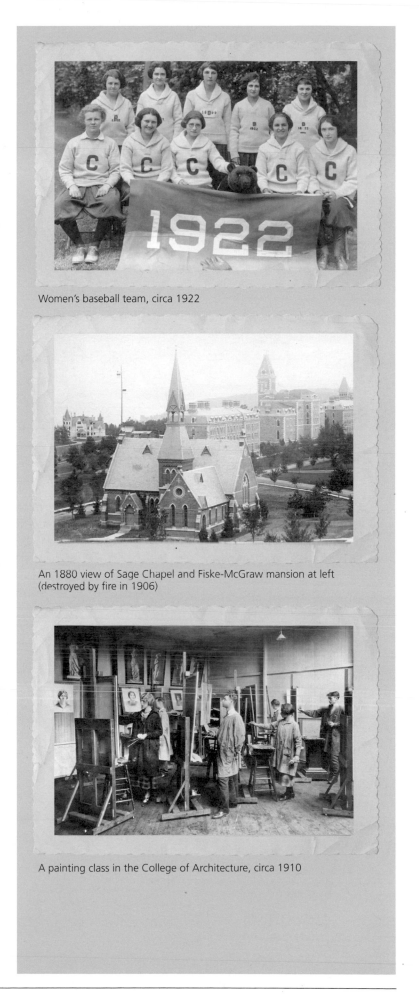

Women's baseball team, circa 1922

An 1880 view of Sage Chapel and Fiske-McGraw mansion at left (destroyed by fire in 1906)

A painting class in the College of Architecture, circa 1910

Cornell University Library Offers More Than Books

Anne Kenney, the Carl A. Kroch University Librarian

Anne Kenney

"... the ideas of a great university and a great library are inextricably linked."

Mind. Body. Soul.
The library feeds all three.

McGraw Tower, the iconic symbol for Cornell University, is the first thing one notices when arriving on campus. It's no coincidence that this imposing clock tower is connected to Uris Library, which, for nearly 70 years, served as the main library on campus. It's also no coincidence that Andrew Dickson White, Cornell's first president, believed that "the ideas of a great university and a great library are inextricably linked." A big-time bibliophile, White donated his own book collection to Cornell and overnight he turned the library into one of the major repositories in nineteenth-century America.

Mind. Body. Soul. The library feeds all three. It's easy to think of the library as a place of the mind. From the very beginning, its chief function has been to assemble and preserve the collective wisdom contained in books, manuscripts, and other documentary forms. But the library also serves a corporeal role. Its physical facilities are destination points, places where an increasing number of Cornellians (more than 4.5 million visits last year) come to gather and consult, learn, study, conduct research, and think. The library is also a source of inspiration that feeds the soul. Curling up in a chair in A.D. White Library overlooking Cayuga Lake on a snowy winter morning, one can

A student studies in the Law Library

be replenished through daydreams. Attend a lecture or view an exhibit and make a connection with things beyond the daily drill. Pull a book off a shelf, listen to a sound recording, or examine an eighteenth-century map and be reminded that existence transcends the 80 years or so we're given.

Students study in the A.D. White Reading Room in Uris Library

Some say there is no longer a need for a research library because everything is online and easily available. But they don't know of Cornell Library and the immense treasures that are located only here, which draw the best and brightest to the university on the Hill, and they don't know that the majority of scholarly online resources are unlocked only through license arrangements managed by the library. They don't know that the faculty ranks the library as the leading indicator of work-life satisfaction, or graduating seniors consistently rank the library as the number-one service on campus, or many students credit the library with saving their grade point averages. When asked to describe the library in one sentence, students from all schools and colleges at Cornell responded. Some of their quotes have become my favorite distillation:

"The last place for thought uninterrupted."

"Peaceful, quiet, caffeine-induced bliss."

"A hushed big bang: behold, the universe expands!"

"Distinguishing signal from noise."

Cornell is in the business of provoking ideas, creativity, and scholarly expression and in training generations of students to address the world's major challenges. As long as the university thrives on the world

of the mind, thought happens. It happens better and more effectively when nourished by the library's resources, services, expertise, and facilities. Andrew Dickson White might fail to appreciate all the changes of the past 150 years, but he would certainly recognize that the library continues to serve as the heart of the university. Come visit us and see for yourself.

FOR MORE INFORMATION
Cornell University Library: library.cornell.edu

A student studies in the ILR School's Catherwood Library

Getting to Know the Faculty

Bill Fry, senior associate dean, College of Agriculture and Life Sciences; professor, Department of Plant Pathology and Plant-Microbe Biology; former dean, University Faculty

Bill Fry

"The faculty is composed of individuals who are sometimes 'otherwise thinking,' always innovative, and extremely active in their teaching and scholarship."

Faculty members at Cornell are very interested in students and want them to succeed. We admire the intelligence, enthusiasm, and industry of Cornell undergrads. We appreciate their challenging questions and their insightful suggestions. We meet students in lecture, discussion groups, class laboratories, and in our own research laboratories. It's exciting to encounter new questions and enthusiasm with each new class. We love when students are truly interested in our discipline.

There are at least three groups of instructors who meet students in classrooms:

• Approximately 1,600 tenure-track faculty members hold the title of assistant professor, associate professor, or professor. Assistant professors are in a probationary situation until they receive tenure—granted typically after a proving period of six years. Assistant professors can be under some noticeable stress while in their probationary status because of the need to demonstrate scholarly accomplishment and do a good job in teaching.

• There are approximately 1,100 lecturers and instructors at Cornell, and some are part time. The major task of lecturers and instructors

is to teach, and they are usually not expected to develop a strong scholarship. They are not eligible for tenure.

• Graduate students often teach lab sections, discussion sessions, and some lecture classes.

The faculty is composed of individuals who are sometimes "otherwise thinking," always innovative, and extremely active in their teaching and scholarship. The Web of Knowledge research platform lists 9,146 scholarly articles contributed by Cornell authors in 2011. In fall 2011 we taught 2,962 undergraduate courses, with students taking a total of 225,550 units, and in spring 2012 we taught 2,942 undergraduate courses, with students taking a total of 214,360 units.

Charles Williamson demonstrates vortex cannons and smoke ring dynamics in his fluid mechanics class

In the 2010–2011 fiscal year, the Ithaca faculty accounted for more than $520 million in research expenditures. In order to continue our research, we submitted more than 2,400 proposals to diverse agencies and foundations.

Bruce Land, senior research associate in electrical and computer engineering, in the laboratory with students

Vicki Bogan, associate professor of applied economics and management, teaching a class

David Feldshuh, professor of theatre, film, and dance, teaching an acting class

Shirley Samuels, professor of English, chair of the Department of History of Art and Visual Studies, and dean of Flora Rose House

Robert Raguso, professor of neurobiology and behavior, collects scents with a student in the Mundy Wildflower Garden, Cornell Plantations

Rosemary Avery, professor of policy analysis and management, has received a Merrill Presidential Teacher Recognition Award 11 times

The Ithaca faculty made 260 disclosures of intellectual property in 2011 and was granted 134 patents based on previous disclosures. Undergraduate students can enrich their collegiate experience and gain insight into a significant aspect of the university if they work with a faculty member in a research setting.

Your son or daughter will interact with a faculty that is very concerned about his or her well-being. Faculty members serve as advisors and want all of their advisees to be successful and happy at Cornell. Occasionally the large size of Cornell presents difficulties for both students and faculty. In some cases it's possible for students to register for courses and never speak to their advisors. Both students and the faculty have recognized this lack of communication as a problem, but it remains an issue because of the automated course registration system. In an attempt to find a solution, the University Faculty Senate (which acts as a voice for the faculty) passed a resolution asking the administration to investigate ways to increase meetings and interactions between students and their faculty advisors.

Several faculty members have contributed to an ongoing discussion about finding ways to lessen undue stress on students. The University Faculty Senate passed two resolutions to help. The first asks that faculty not surprise students with additional assignments immediately

before or after breaks in the semester. The second adjusts the academic calendar by adding an additional break into the spring semester and repositioning the current spring break into the middle of the longest stretch of the calendar.

It's very important for students to get to know the faculty. They can do this by attending office hours, discussion sessions, and review sessions and by working in a research program. In developing these connections, it's important for students to remember that the faculty is very diverse, and each faculty member has a responsibility for research as well as teaching. What works for one may not work for another. Some are more devoted to teaching than are others. Most faculty members are very busy and work long hours. Nonetheless, they will bend over backward to accommodate a student who is serious about learning the subject matter. Faculty are interested in all students— not just the ones who are at the top of the class.

FOR MORE INFORMATION
The dean of faculty is responsible for academic integrity. View the "Essential Guide to Academic Integrity at Cornell": newstudentprograms.cornell.edu/academicintegritypamphlet.pdf

Our View of One Cornell

Laura Brown, senior vice provost, undergraduate education, Cornell University; the John Wendell Anderson Chair, Department of English, College of Arts and Sciences

Laura Brown

"For many students, participation in community engagement—locally or globally—motivates their learning and prepares them for future engagement with the world beyond Cornell."

Your student's academic experience at Cornell will take place primarily within his or her major department and college, where he or she will take classes to master a field of study, engage with peers in course work and informal study activities, receive advice from faculty members and professional advisors, and perhaps complete a capstone project or thesis that makes an original contribution to a discipline. Our departments and programs are committed to making your student's academic experience as a specialist in a particular field as intellectually exciting and educationally rewarding as possible by supplying a curriculum that prepares him or her at each stage of course work for increasing depth of inquiry and by providing personal and institutional guidance at every turn.

At Cornell your student will also find academic opportunities that extend beyond his or her major. And for many students, these experiences will be the most meaningful, memorable, and important of their college years. In fact, it's likely that you and your student were already aware of the special benefits, like these, that come with attending Cornell University. We know that numerous students choose Cornell for the chance to take part in research with leading scientists and scholars, the opportunity to travel abroad for study or

service, the ability to serve the local or global community, the prospect of a residential experience guided by involved faculty who live and dine with students and who integrate learning and living on campus, or the possibility of taking courses that cross the broad expanse of Cornell's academic offerings and link fundamental discovery with practical application. All of these opportunities draw together the multiple strengths of the university into One Cornell.

While the Office of the Vice Provost for Undergraduate Education works to help your student master the fundamentals of his or her chosen major, it also works to make that mastery more meaningful and relevant by placing it in broader contexts. We believe that these academic avenues enable your student to make the most of a Cornell education, and we strongly urge our students to pursue them. Undergraduate research, for instance, has become a key component of undergraduate education, especially at universities like Cornell where cutting-edge science and scholarship are fundamental to our institutional mission. Students who participate in research actually see the creation of knowledge—their learning extends beyond the outcomes that are presented in the classroom into the realm of creativity itself. And a research experience builds students' connections with faculty in ways that also extend beyond the interactions of the classroom or the context of academic advising. The faculty-student research partnership results in mentoring often based on a connection that supports close and sustained academic and career guidance.

Left: *Sweeping Away Ignorance at the Rural Qingzhen (Halal) Market* in Najiaying, Yunnan, China. (Photo by Lesley Turnbull, a Fulbright-Hays Doctoral Dissertation Research Abroad Fellowship recipient)

And in many areas, student researchers connect with peers in their labs and research groups, forming communities that become sources of significant support and satisfaction. We also know that participation in research plays a key role in supporting our underrepresented students by inspiring academic experiences and successes that are enhanced through this kind of intellectual engagement. Cornell's Office of Undergraduate Research, an academic initiative of the Office of the Vice Provost for Undergraduate Education, encourages undergraduate research by connecting students with faculty across the colleges and schools, inspiring new partnerships in all fields, including the arts and humanities, and promoting the work of campus-wide student research organizations.

International education has never been more immediately applicable to our students' research, learning, and future careers. Cornell students are now preparing to be global citizens, and we support a range of opportunities for international education, from the semester abroad model managed by Cornell Abroad and various exchange programs operated by the schools and colleges, to global service learning and research trips designed by individual faculty members and programs. In fact, international education has become priority at Cornell. With President Skorton's encouragement, we are redesigning our study abroad programs to help more students take advantage of opportunities for global engagement. We are creating initiatives that enable students to pursue research in specific locations abroad, and we are modeling programs that combine international education and global service learning. Engaged Learning + Research, supported by the Office of the Vice Provost for Undergraduate Education, provides grants to students for global service learning and international research and advises faculty who design these programs.

More broadly, Engaged Learning + Research reaches across Cornell's colleges and schools and touches nearly all of Cornell's undergraduate students. Since its founding, Cornell has held to the fundamental tenet that education and social needs intersect. Today, the transformative connection between education and society is an integral dimension of the university's mission. We believe distinguishing hallmarks of Cornell graduates are that their learning is linked to the experiences of service and stewardship, and their knowledge is grounded in the connection between intellect and practical solutions to social problems. For many students, participation in community engagement—locally or globally—motivates their learning and prepares them for future engagement with the world beyond Cornell. Engaged Learning + Research serves as an interdisciplinary, university-wide resource for students and faculty seeking to apply their studies to help support communities in Ithaca, New York State, the United States, and the world. Student ambassadors in Engaged

Paul Merrill, faculty-in-residence, senior lecturer in music, and director of jazz ensembles, working with students / Parvine Toorawa, a member of the faculty family-in-residence, in Mews Hall / Yufen Lee Frances Mehta, professor of Chinese language in the Department of Asian Studies and faculty-in-residence for Court-Kay-Bauer Hall, hosts a Taste of India Social in the residence lounge

Learning + Research are eager to help students find experiences, programs, and courses that match their interests and fields of study.

The opportunity to interact with faculty outside the classroom—in the residence halls and elsewhere on campus—allows students to share in the intellectual community that makes them true learners. The Office of the Vice Provost for Undergraduate Education supports faculty programs in the residence halls on North Campus and West Campus that enable our best teachers to contribute to Cornell's educational mission by living in the residence halls or by dining regularly in the student dining facilities. The formal and informal exchanges with these faculty members give our students a chance to sample a range of educational opportunities beyond the formal curriculum, including research, public service, and experiential learning. Our faculty-in-residence develop personal connections with students, helping them feel comfortable with their professors and creating mentoring networks outside the classroom.

And we are eager to make your student's education cross disciplinary, like Cornell itself. We want your student's learning experience to reflect Cornell's unique range of academic opportunities—in areas of study as well as in basic and applied approaches to knowledge. Cornell students may take courses in any undergraduate college and may minor in any field of study at the university. We offer a curriculum of cross-disciplinary courses, called University Courses, that highlights the distinctive character of Cornell and that provides a shared educational experience for our undergraduates. These courses are team-taught and emphasize open dialogue on topics of current concern. They give students a wider context for their specialized studies, involve them with peers from across the university, create a broad community of learners that bridges distances between our distinct colleges and schools, provide occasions for innovative teaching, and create an environment in which students and faculty experience Cornell as one university.

We know that undergraduate research, international education, public service, living-learning programs, and cross-disciplinary study contribute to student success, satisfaction, and engagement. We very much hope your student will find some programs of interest among these cross-campus initiatives. Cornell offers the best of higher education in placing your student's specialized study in the broader context of our wide-ranging intellectual community and our encompassing academic mission on campus and in the world—the context of One Cornell.

FOR MORE INFORMATION
Engaged Learning + Research: elr.cornell.edu

"International education has never been more immediately applicable to our students' research, learning, and future careers."

Top (left to right): Cornell students joined Indian students in transplanting rice seedlings during a class field trip to India / The Judith Reppy Institute for Peace and Conflict Studies organized a panel discussion on terrorism with Cornell professors Matt Evangelista, Barry Strauss, and Peter J. Katzenstein / The Global Health Program launched a nine week, service-learning initiative for undergraduates in Moshi, Tanzania / Photo by Bob Beazley, a Mario Einaudi Center for International Studies travel grant recipient, who traveled along the Buddhist pilgrimage route in Tibet to collect mushrooms and fungi used in traditional Chinese medicine

The Freedom to Take Academic Risks

Marcus Loo '77, MD '81, clinical professor, Department of Urology, Weill Cornell Medical College

Marcus Loo '77, MD '81

"The course I took in biophysics was, at the time, way outside my comfort zone, as I had only taken high school biology—but it transformed my life."

Although I graduated from Cornell decades ago, I have remained connected to my alma mater in many ways over the years. I am also a proud Cornell parent. As such, the perspective I would like to offer is that of an alumnus and parent.

When I arrived on the Cornell campus in 1973, I surely felt I was going to major in aerospace engineering. Having grown up in the 1960s, I was captivated by the exploration of space and the phenomenal achievement of landing a man on the moon. However, over the next three years I became interested in materials science, applied physics, polymer chemistry, and economics. In contrast to my early aspiration, I ended up majoring in electrical engineering, doing research in biophysics, and then going to medical school. Today I am a urologist and have a practice in New York's Chinatown.

With that experience in mind, the first piece of advice I can offer is to avoid asking your son or daughter what he or she is going to major in—because, in all likelihood, it will change many times. With seven undergraduate schools and colleges as well as thousands of courses of study to choose from, Cornell students are exposed to a rich and extremely diverse learning environment befitting one of the world's best research universities.

Left: Students in a class in the School of Industrial and Labor Relations

One of the most distinctive aspects of a Cornell education is the opportunity for students to be exposed to so many domains of inquiry and disciplines of study. As a result, there is a tremendous amount of interdisciplinary research. Students learn the importance and power of developing collaborations when trying to find novel solutions to problems.

Marcus Loo at his Cornell graduation in 1977

Cornell faculty members are extraordinarily passionate about teaching and research, so they welcome self-motivated students to participate and learn how new knowledge is created. Every student at Cornell has the opportunity to be inspired and mentored by a faculty member. For many, as was the case for me, this is in an invaluable experience.

My next piece of advice is to encourage your student to take some risk in his or her course of study and challenge himself or herself academically. The course I took in biophysics was, at the time, way outside my comfort zone, as I had only taken high school biology—but it transformed my life. I enjoyed the course so much I spent two years working in a biophysics laboratory and was encouraged by my professor to think about a career in medicine.

For some students, the size of the Cornell campus can be somewhat overwhelming. With thousands of acres of land and more than 17,000 undergraduate and graduate students, navigating this living and learning environment can be a daunting challenge. Another thought to consider is how you can make a large university community seem smaller. All first-year students have a common shared living experience on North Campus. In subsequent years, Cornell gives students the freedom to choose to live in smaller groups, off-campus housing, the Greek system of fraternities and sororities, or one of the residential houses on West Campus. Regarding the enormous size of the campus and how best to get around, I can only say that during my time on campus I had a bicycle. I found the challenges of getting to early morning classes in the cold Ithaca winters part of the character-building aspect of a Cornell education.

It is my strong belief that what students choose to do in their free time at Cornell will help shape their future. Beyond the classroom there are so many extracurricular opportunities for students to explore. There are nearly 1,000 student organizations and clubs. The campus is full of student-initiated activity that pursues passions in athletics, music, dance, writing, community service, and the building of award-winning autonomous submersible vehicles—to name a few. The diversity of student interest is tremendous, and each student organization helps to educate, inform, and enrich the entire community. Participation in extracurricular activities enables students to interact in smaller groups, develop friendships, test leadership and organizational skills, and allows for a more fulfilling student life experience. This is not to suggest that all Cornell students should not strive for a balance in their lives, which would include time for sleep, good nutrition, and exercise.

The academic program at Cornell has not changed since I was a student. It is still very rigorous and extremely challenging. This can create a fairly stressful environment for students. That said, I would recommend not asking your son or daughter about his or her grades. Admission to Cornell is validation of your student's intellectual capabilities, and as we all know, course grades are not necessarily a reflection of what has been learned. A wonderful aspect of a Cornell education is the chance to explore, find challenges, engage passionately in activities, and interact with a diverse student body and faculty. To be completely focused on grades may constrain opportunities to grow. If your student wants you to know about grades, he or she will tell you. Cornell has a host of resources, including academic advising, peer and professional counseling, and career placement services—to which students have free access. Much of this book is devoted to helping families understand the many resources available to students who are experiencing difficulties with their transition to life at Cornell.

The phrase that is often used when describing the Cornell experience is "freedom with responsibility." Students are allowed wide latitude to choose what kind of living environment works best for them as well as the curriculum of study that is best suited to their interests. This freedom of choice comes with the understanding that students have to be responsible for their decisions and be active participants in the living and learning community.

Students taking advantage of Cornell's bike share on a crisp autumn afternoon

Popshop is a new space for Cornell students and Ithaca residents to engage in scheduled programs and chance encounters, discuss their entrepreneurial ideas, organize meetings for their startups, and receive guidance and support from experienced entrepreneurs on campus

Students blend their own blueberry smoothies and win fabulous prizes at Unleash Your Blueberry Brain Power at North Star Dining

Students gather at the banquet held at the end of Ramadan

Engineering students test the Cornell University Autonomous Underwater Vehicle in Teagle Hall's swimming pool

The 144th Cornell University Commencement and Procession (2012)

In sum, my last piece of advice is: let go. There is no question that there will be times at Cornell (hopefully not often) when disappointments and mistakes will happen. Students need to advocate for themselves, learn how to resolve differences, and overcome hardships. However, you should trust that Cornell has invested tremendous resources to help students with their physical, emotional, and mental health and their academic needs.

I believe that a Cornell education provides not only an encompassing preparation for lifelong learning but also personal fulfillment. There is an emphasis in the ethos of Cornell for service and public engagement, which students are exposed to in so many ways. Cornell students learn to appreciate the intersection of theory and practice. Many of the challenges confronting our society and the world will necessitate novel and innovative interdisciplinary solutions. Cornell students, from their activities in and out of the classroom, are well prepared to take on these challenges and be responsible global citizens. The time I spent in Ithaca was truly a transformational one. I have great anticipation that this will be true for your family as well.

My very last recommendation is to learn to sing the Cornell University Alma Mater. Every major Cornell event, including Commencement, ends with it.

So Many Choices, So Little Time

David N. DeVries, associate dean, undergraduate education, College of Arts and Sciences

David DeVries

"Andrew White, Ezra Cornell, and their first faculty colleagues believed that the most effective way to put those ideas in action was to create an academic atmosphere that valued freedom."

Looking back over the first 30 years of the university that he helped found with Ezra Cornell, Andrew Dickson White, Cornell University's first president, observed that there were two "permeating ideas" informing the university's approach to education. "First, the development of the individual . . . as a being intellectual [and] moral. Secondly, bringing the powers . . . thus developed to bear usefully upon society."

Of course, from the first, those permeating ideas applied equally to women as to men, since Cornell was coeducational from the start. More to the point though, Andrew White, Ezra Cornell, and their first faculty colleagues believed that the most effective way to put those ideas in action was to create an academic atmosphere that valued freedom. In a similar review of the first 35 years of Cornell's history, in 1906, Thomas Frederick Crane (Cornell's first professor of romance languages, first chair of the Department of Romance Languages, first dean of the College of Arts and Sciences, and first person to serve as an interim president of the university) reflected on what he called the "educational ideals of

Andrew Dickson White

Cornell University": freedom from traditional influences, recognition of the equality of all fields of study, and seriousness of purpose and maturity of its students.

The first enabled us to break away from the rigid, old-fashioned college curriculum with the single degree; the second led us to broaden our courses of study; and the third to enlarge the freedom of choice of studies.

But the freedom presented its own problems, chief among them: how was a student to choose wisely? By 1906, all of Cornell's colleges had developed a method for students enrolling in their courses that required each student to meet with the dean of the college in order to review their choices and then the college's registrar in order to complete the registration process. When the student population still numbered in the hundreds, such a method was (barely) possible. But in the largest college, the College of Arts and Sciences, even by 1906 the numbers of students made the process unwieldy, and a system was developed that required students to meet with faculty members regularly, especially during registration times. (It is worth noting that the first dean and first registrar in the College of Arts and Sciences

Left: Students turn in homework assignments and take their seats in Baker 200 for Chemistry 2090

became well-known enough to figure in the "Cornell Fight Song": Thomas Fredrick (T.F.) Crane and David Hoy, aka Teefy and Davy. Just attend enough Cornell sporting events and you will learn the song!)

Now, in the early decades of the twenty-first century, the choices in terms of courses, majors, minors, opportunities for independent research with faculty, and the wide range of academic experiences have grown far beyond anything White and Crane could have imagined. Students coming to the "hill above Cayuga's waters" today quite literally have thousands of courses from which to choose. Within the seven undergraduate colleges, there are dozens of majors; there are also dozens of minors that are available to students no matter which college is their home college. How to choose among that rich array of intellectual experience can be daunting for students. The system of advising that T.F. Crane helped to create has grown along with the curriculum and opportunities at Cornell. Faculty in each of Cornell's undergraduate colleges are involved in advising students. Beyond the faculty, each of the colleges has professional staff serving as support for students as they make their ways through Cornell's varied and challenging curricula.

There is, however, no standard model for advising across Cornell's seven undergraduate colleges. The colleges do share a commitment to helping students become their own best advocates, helping students to take responsibility for their own education so that they get their

academic legs beneath them and walk confidently into their futures as members of the far-flung and loyal Cornell alumni body. Andrew Dickson White's permeating ideas that education should develop a student's entire being and that the purpose of that education is to prepare young people to go forth and do good for their communities, their nations, the world—those ideas continue to animate the work that faculty and staff do at Cornell on behalf of students.

Crane's faith in what he called the "seriousness of purpose and maturity of [Cornell's] students" has been passed on to those of us who carry on his tasks as dean, faculty member, staff advisor. We assume that Cornell students are mature enough and serious enough to shoulder the responsibilities of adult life imbued with a desire to serve purposes larger than themselves or their immediate needs and wants. We provide instruction, guidance, support. We measure our success as advisors by the extent to which our students are able to surprise us with the reach and scope of their ambitions, with the manifold ways that they fulfill White's desire that students leave the hill with their powers developed so that they bear usefully on society. Of course, by "usefully" White meant a great deal more than amassing fortunes—as he put it, he sought to guard Cornell University from "the men to whom 'Gain is God, and Gunnybags his Prophet.'" White believed that creating and sustaining a great university was a patriotic duty, since "the most important duty of our republic is to develop the best minds it possesses for the best service in all its fields of high intellectual activity."

Fiber science and apparel design students in the College of Human Ecology sewing room

Top (left to right): A graduate student in the College of Engineering works with the walking Cornell Ranger Robot / Students in the School of Industrial and Labor Relations in class / Architecture, Art, and Planning students prepare the *Unpacking the Nano* exhibition at the Johnson Museum of Art / Students in the School of Hotel Administration attend a seminar on classified châteaux wines from the 1998 vintage, delivered by guest speaker Jean-Michel Cazes / Celeste Marie Falcon '11, who studied plant science with a concentration in plant breeding and genetics in the College of Agriculture and Life Sciences, wrote a senior honors thesis that mapped the genes responsible for inulin content in wheat and discussed the plausibility of breeding for increased inulin content / College of Arts and Sciences music students Alex Huth '13 and Diana Rypkema '13

ANNA HERFORTH

IN ITHACA AND AROUND THE WORLD

International education has never been more immediately applicable to our students' research, learning, and future careers.

—Brendan O'Brien

Above: Engineering students on the AguaClara team bring clean drinking water to Hondurans

Left: The CU Winds ensemble in Costa Rica

My Opportunity to Repay International Hospitality

Brendan O'Brien, associate dean of students, Cornell University; director, International Students and Scholars Office

Brendan O'Brien

"We cherish our international students and we want to do everything we can to make their stays as productive and fulfilling as possible."

I have been working at the International Students and Scholars Office (ISSO) at Cornell University since 1989, and it has been a great honor. In any given year, Cornell hosts approximately 4,300 international students, and it is a pleasure to work with them. I learn from them every day, and their presence greatly enriches our university. The diversity of ideas, talents, and perspectives that international students bring to Cornell is immeasurable. We are grateful to the Cornell parents for sending their children to the university.

The International Students and Scholars Office plays an important role in supporting our international students. The mission of our office, which was founded in 1936, is to assist individual international students and foreign academic staff and their families by advising them concerning federal immigration, tax, and labor regulations and by providing counseling on personal, academic, and cultural matters. In addition, we try to promote cross-cultural awareness in the Cornell community through educational programming such as orientation, cultural adjustment, and cross-cultural communication.

Left: The 2012 welcome reception for international students and families

We have 10 full-time staff members who are dedicated to serving our international students and visiting scholars. Our staff recognizes the importance of international students and educational exchange in bringing people together and making the world a safer place. The words of former President Dwight Eisenhower, spoken in 1958, have never been more relevant: "Information and education are powerful forces in the support of peace. Just as war begins in the minds of men, so does peace."

We cherish our international students, and we want to do everything we can to make their stays as productive and fulfilling as possible. As we serve our students, we are sometimes motivated by the broad goals of world peace and international understanding.

Students socializing at the Center for Intercultural Dialogue

"Our staff recognizes the importance of international students and educational exchange in bringing people together and making the world a safer place."

Various members of student clubs and organizations enjoy a night of food and entertainment during the 8th Annual Asia Night

At other times, our motivations are more personal. My main motivation to serve this population comes from personal experiences studying, working, and traveling abroad. As a young man, I was fortunate to have had the opportunity to study in Kenya, Israel, and France. I also spent a year teaching English in Taiwan and have traveled to numerous other countries. Wherever I have gone, I have been the recipient of incredible hospitality, kindness, and generosity.

Brendan O'Brien during a semester abroad in Kenya, 1980

I will never forget my experiences studying in Nairobi, Kenya in 1980. I was a junior in college and it was my first time outside the United States. On one of my first days there, I went out in search of a post office to mail a letter home to my parents informing them that I had arrived safely. I wasn't exactly certain of the post office location, so I stopped a Kenyan man to seek his assistance. I was immediately touched by his warmth and concern. He didn't simply give me directions; he walked me to the post office and then proceeded to invite me to his home for lunch and to meet his family. To this day, I am grateful to him for his hospitality. But more importantly, I am grateful to him for helping me to see the world a little differently. Since that time, many people have shared their culture with me and have shown me great kindness. Although I can never directly repay all of that kindness, I am fortunate to be in a position at Cornell where I can make a small repayment as I try to welcome others to the university and to the United States.

Brendan O'Brien with his wife, Sachiko Funaba, and daughters, Mina and Saya, traveling in Osaka, Japan

My other motivation is also quite personal. I became a father in 2004 and now have two daughters aged ten and six. Like all parents throughout the world, I want the best for my children. I want them to be safe and happy, but I understand that their safety and happiness cannot be absolutely guaranteed. At times, we must put our children in the trust of others. I remember the anxious feelings I had when my older daughter got on the school bus for the first time. I knew it was not necessary, but I gave the bus driver a special reminder to drive safely. When my daughters are older and ready to pursue education at a university away from home, I want them to be well cared for by staff and faculty who are committed to their personal growth and well-being. I am certain that other parents share those same desires as they send their children to Cornell. International parents feel those desires more intensely as they send their children across the globe to a foreign country.

When you send your student to Cornell, we are entrusted with an awesome responsibility. On behalf of the entire staff of ISSO, I promise you that we will do our best to fulfill that responsibility. I encourage you and your student to reach out to me or any other ISSO staff member if there is anything we can do to be of assistance. We are anxious to serve.

FOR MORE INFORMATION
ISSO: isso.cornell.edu

A group discusses *Homer and Langley* by E.L. Doctorow, the book chosen for the 2011 New Student Reading Project

Scenes from the South Asia Shaadi, organized by the Society for India, the Pakistani Student Association, and the Bengali Student Association

Our Daughter's Journey to Cornell

Georgia Garinois-Melenikiotou, senior vice president, corporate marketing, The Estée Lauder Companies, Inc.

Philippe Garinois, vice president, Deleplanque & Cie, France

Georgia Garinois-Melenikiotou and
Philippe Garinois

"We went to the Cornell campus in late August.
We were all together; the four of us.
Philippe and I were so proud, yet so emotional."

A Greek mother, Georgia, a French father, Philippe, and two amazing children. Laura-India is our youngest. Alessandro is our first-born and two years older than Laura-India. We are all four very different, yet so similar. We are an ordinary family that was made through extraordinary circumstances. Both parents in business, not as present physically as we would have liked to be, yet overwhelmingly present both in terms of setting values and creating an emotional net of security, love, and self-confidence for our children. As we all grew up and created an atypical family, our motto was "one for four, four for one." We lived in six countries, yet half of the time one of the two parents had to commute. We spoke French and Greek at home, yet the kids were going to a British school. We all loved our summers in Greece and our autumns in France, yet we loved projects. We all worked very hard, yet we enjoyed so much art, food, and life.

Laura-India always had a very strong hand, remarkably personal style, and also a very strong head. When she was 12 she told us she wanted to do something with design, creativity, shaping lives, and changing the world. Architecture seemed a natural decision for her. The United States was also a natural decision, although the French and other European architecture schools are also very good. She got

Laura-India at six years old in London; "one for four, four for one"

to know about Cornell architecture through a passionate student, Ujjiji, and fell in love with the school after spending one summer there the year before her graduation. Everything was perfect for her, and it was meant to be. The diversity and international student body, the challenging and forward thinking faculty, the possibility for a professional degree (a normal practice in Europe but not the norm in the United States), the beautiful campus in the middle of amazing

Left: Laura-India Garinois '17 on campus at Dragon Day 2013

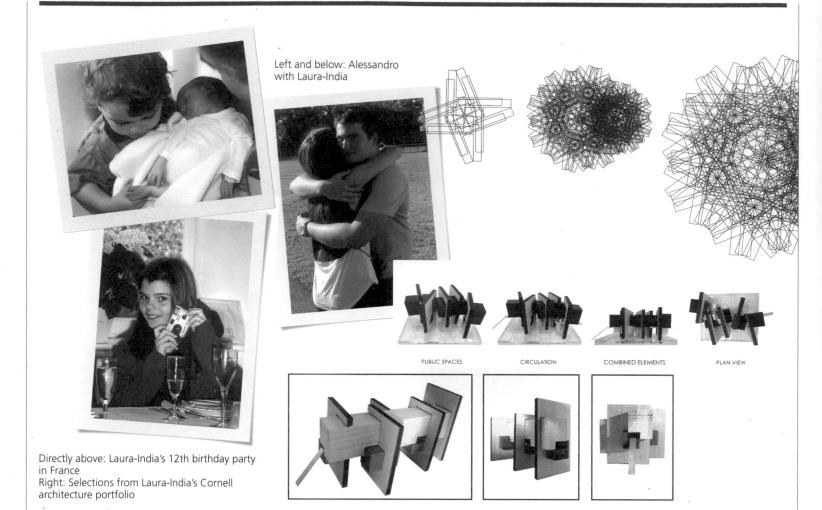

Left and below: Alessandro with Laura-India

Directly above: Laura-India's 12th birthday party in France

Right: Selections from Laura-India's Cornell architecture portfolio

PUBLIC SPACES   CIRCULATION   COMBINED ELEMENTS   PLAN VIEW

natural beauty, and, most importantly, Cornell's Department of Architecture marked her forever. For Laura, the summer school at the College of Architecture, Art, and Planning (AAP) was perhaps one of her most significant, life-changing experiences. When she came back, she was determined to get accepted.

I was concerned because AAP had a reputation for being very selective and for making its students work very hard. But, above all, I was worried about Laura. She was so much in love with Cornell and Ithaca that I was concerned about how she would feel if she was not accepted. The most intense moment in her life was the last five minutes of the countdown for the online results—she was accepted for early decision. She felt very blessed to have been accepted.

We went to the Cornell campus in late August. We were all together; the four of us. Philippe and I were so proud, yet so emotional. We were impressed by the college's amazing resources, the faculty, the international student body, and the academic performance and research projects, which all strive to "make an impact, not just an impression, in the world of tomorrow." We loved the fact that Ithaca was both a big college town and had natural beauty. I was particularly impressed by the beautiful trees on the campus. The academic level, the natural beauty, and the university's location are so perfect for Laura.

Sometimes I am concerned about the pressures of the workload and the competitiveness of the college because Laura-India is still my baby. But she is so happy with her college and with herself—she is so thankful and proud to be part of Cornell's student body. She has learned so much; she is almost a different person. She is more mature, she feels comfortable competing, and she is confident about her ideas. We are so proud of her.

We thank Cornell for its contributions in making our beautiful girl a wholesome young adult.

Laura-India and brother, Alessandro, walking into Milstein Hall

My Fortunate Odyssey
Laura-India Garinois '17, an application essay for Cornell Summer College

Four education systems, two nationalities, two religions, and five languages: what does all this make of me? I was born to a Greek-Orthodox mother and a French-Catholic father and I have been fortunate to already be exposed to various educational systems: British, Greek, French, and American. All this made me more adaptable, more resilient, and love change. It formed my character but did not change who I really am as a person: determined yet a dreamer, passionate and deep about issues that matter to me—such as protecting the weaker and making an impact, yet enjoying a good laugh with my friends.

My interests all tend to revolve around humanity. Over the last three years, I have been elected class president three times in high school. This consists of representing my class, defending every classmate objectively, and resolving problems of everyday school life. This experience allowed me to strengthen my organization skills and forged the sense of responsibility that comes with representing other people's interests. During the eighth and ninth grades I also introduced, with my brother, a program called Love in a Box, which consists of Christmas gifts in shoeboxes for less-privileged children. This is a personal way of giving to others, rather than writing a check. Love in a Box has been personally rewarding to me, knowing that many less-privileged children will smile on Christmas day.

My exposure to several education systems not only gave me a deeper understanding of different cultures, but also allowed me to experience distinctive perspectives of the world through the eyes of a child. At five years old, I joined a British school in Paris without speaking a word of English. I was able to observe without talking for a year. Three years later we moved to England. Although I found the move challenging at first, I quickly adapted to it, forging my little British accent and dry sense of humor. At 12, I enrolled in a French school. My integration to the French system was tough, but extremely valuable; I learned how to use the rigor of the system to my advantage. Since last September, I have lived in New York—a new challenge and an amazing opportunity. I am attracted by the openness and flexibility of the system that allows for many routes to success—so different from the French elitist and the Greek purist approach.

Diversity of views also forged my creative nature. I've grown up with deep love for art. I've always known that my career would revolve around it, but I remained unsure for several years. My dreams evolved from being a pianist, writer, or painter, to a graphic designer. But for the past five years now, there is a certainty in my life: I want to be an architect! In fact, every day I am constantly drawn more and more to the field of architecture. What attracts me is how it combines different fields such as art, history, math, engineering, sociology, business, and politics. What makes me passionate, however, is its magic to beautifully transform everyday life to make it better and timeless.

I was fortunate to live in major cities that influenced me greatly: the unexpected combination of old and postmodern architecture of London, the purity of the Greek classical architecture, the elegance of Paris with its unique architectural beauty and history, and now, New York, one of the world's centers of architecture, have all been my inspiration. They allowed me to experience a wonderful balance of history and future, tradition and modernity, big city and small communities. The history of architecture and design courses I took at Parsons in New York and in Paris at the Columbia summer school have intensified my passion for architecture.

In truth, I understood what it means to be an architect only after I was exposed to real-life work experiences. During spring break of ninth grade, I worked for DDB, an advertising agency in Paris; in eleventh grade, for an architect's office in Athens; and last June, at the *Architectural Digest* magazine in New York. Those experiences made me realize how much I enjoy tasks that require the creative manipulation and coordination of visual and copy elements to effectively communicate a message. I also enjoyed thoroughly listening and developing a deeper insight on client's needs. Finally, all this made me realize that success in creative professions also encompasses pragmatic skills, such as scheduling, cost estimating, and client administration. But most importantly, after those experiences, I am certain that architecture will be my vocation, a Latin word that means an occupation to which one feels specially drawn or for which one is suited. Architecture for me is a mixture of science, art, and poetry and the chance to connect with others through the most important part of being—their space.

My life so far has been a very fortunate odyssey. The journey made me more open, more compassionate, more creative, and more ingenious. It also armed me with the confidence that everything is possible, if I really want it.

Opportunities for Public Engagement and Service Learning

Leonardo Vargas-Méndez, executive director, Cornell Public Service Center
Richard Kiely, PhD '02, director, Engaged Learning + Research

Leonardo Vargas-Méndez

"Education either functions as an instrument to facilitate integration of the younger generation into the logic of the present system and bring about conformity, or it becomes the practice of freedom, the means by which men and women deal critically and creatively with reality and discover how to participate in the transformation of their world."
—Paulo Freire

As educator and philosopher Paulo Freire reminds us, public engagement is fundamental to a citizen's work. The combination of community engagement and education creates a critically informed, well trained, and socially conscious citizen. Public engagement has been at the core of Cornell's history, tradition, and education since its inception. As a New York State land-grant university, Cornell has developed an array of high-impact pedagogies to connect students, faculty, and staff with larger communities throughout Ithaca, the Southern Tier, New York State, the nation, and the world.

Students, faculty, staff, and community members can take advantage of well-established institutional vehicles for public engagement such as Cornell Cooperative Extension, which reaches all counties in the state of New York, and the Cornell Public Service Center, which organizes and mobilizes thousands of students and faculty members in curricular and co-curricular community service-learning projects in collaboration with hundreds of community organizations and government agencies. In addition, Engaged Learning + Research, a recently created university-wide center, focuses its community-based learning and research efforts in four main areas: pedagogy and curriculum, research, community development, and institutional change. The center provides consultation services to faculty, departments, colleges, staff, community-based organizations, and students who wish to develop new courses, learn innovative teaching and research strategies, and create and sustain meaningful working relationships with community partners across Ithaca, New York City, and beyond. The plethora of public engagement activities, resources, and programs supported by these organizations bring Cornell's land-grant mission to life by offering students the opportunity to make a positive difference in the world during their tenure at Cornell and preparing them to be future leaders and change-makers.

As students arrive on campus, they find a rich and diverse set of opportunities for community engagement and experiential learning. Pre-orientation programs challenge incoming students to engage with their surroundings and to build relationships with the local community. Opportunities range from one-time, student-led community service activities to sustained community engagement throughout the year. Students can enroll in interdisciplinary service-learning courses or participate in community-based research that enhances their learning. The Public Service Center and Engaged Learning + Research are establishing multiple pathways for student engagement, and also mapping those experiential pathways to expand Cornell students' creative, collaborative, and reflective leadership capacities in order to act in a socially responsive and empathic manner.

Left: Students at Ithaca's Northeast Elementary School learn about reptiles from Howard Evans (out of the frame on the left, holding the snakeskin), professor emeritus of veterinary biomedical sciences

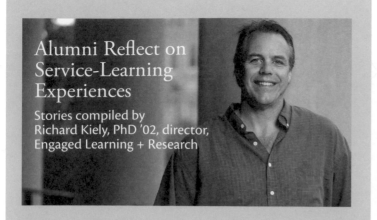

Alumni Reflect on Service-Learning Experiences

Stories compiled by
Richard Kiely, PhD '02, director,
Engaged Learning + Research

Students at Hospicare in Ithaca, participating in the Pre-Orientation Service Trips program

Laura Marie Romeo '09

I transferred to the College of Human Ecology in 2006 and graduated in 2009 with a major in human biology, health, and society. After graduation, I participated in a year of service with City Year New York (an AmeriCorps program), completed my master degree in child life at Bank Street College of Education, and became a certified child life specialist.

I was a Cornell Urban Scholar and an Iscol Scholar during the summer of 2008. I feel comfortable saying that this service-learning experience shaped my Cornell experience and changed my life. My internship in the Cornell Urban Scholars Program (CUSP) was at New York–Presbyterian Hospital/Weill Cornell Medical Center in the Child Life Program. I fell in love with the field and am now pursuing it in my career as an employee at the same hospital. CUSP did much more for me besides set my career on a fast track. I learned so much about social justice during my pre- and post-CUSP classes. I become passionate about bringing social change to our community and dedicated my senior year to helping reform our bias-related incident protocols in the residence halls and on campus. With the skills I was taught in my CUSP classes, I was able to convince Residential Programs to alter their bias-related incident protocol in the dorms and brought light to the bias-related incident response program on campus (news. cornell.edu/stories/Feb09/BiasResponse.html). Even after graduating, professionals at Cornell are still asking me for the papers I wrote in my CUSP classes that focus on the research I did about bias-related incidents. It's truly amazing!

I was already very involved in campus life as a resident advisor, research assistant, dance fitness instructor, and founder of the hip-hop dance group Break Free, but CUSP made me feel like I had a real purpose at Cornell. When people ask me what my best Cornell experience was, I always say that it's my service-learning experiences, hands down. I feel like my service-learning pre- and post-CUSP classes were the best classes I took because I was making a difference in the world while I was taking them. It encouraged me to do a year of service upon graduation and to follow my passions of advocating for infants, children, and their families experiencing traumatic life events. I do sincerely hope that current students still have the opportunities I had to engage in service learning. In my opinion, you can't call a school an advocate for public engagement and social justice if it doesn't have these types of programs and service-learning classes.

Cornell students are invited to participate in highly challenging engaged learning activities such as internships in New York City; Albany, New York; Washington, D.C.; Rome; or London. They can also take part in a global service-learning program in Nicaragua, Belize, Honduras, Tanzania, or Ghana, or simply join hundreds of students in the Alternative Spring Break service trips to New Orleans, New York City, parts of Upstate New York, Orlando, or West

"Engaged students at Cornell gain the knowledge, skills, and habits for lifelong learning and active citizenship in our society."

Virginia. Students may choose to become a member of one of the dozens of student-led public service organizations that have long-standing partnerships with human service and government agencies in Tompkins County and the Southern Tier. They work closely with local residents, professionals, and community leaders to address important community problems such as hunger relief, homelessness, urban and rural poverty, food security, public safety, economic development, and health. Students can also team up with others to create their own service organizations to address a youth, senior citizen, or family advocacy issue, and also apply for grants established through a close collaboration between the Student Assembly and the Public Service Center. Partnerships with the Ithaca, Newfield, Spencer-Van Etten, Elmira, and Groton City school districts and the Ithaca Youth Bureau provide hundreds of service-learning opportunities for Cornell students who want to get involved in mentorship, tutoring, other academic enrichment activities, or projects with K–12 students in local schools.

In addition to offering abundant opportunities for students to make meaningful connections with communities on and off campus, the Public Service Center and Engaged Learning + Research programs promote critical reflection. Students continuously learn through service and engagement with community collaborators and come to appreciate, understand, and value diverse communities and their individual and collective knowledge. Community engaged learning pedagogies are, first and foremost, teaching and learning exchanges among participants where everyone is a co-teacher and co-learner. They reflect on factors that influence complex social problems, develop their civic leadership abilities, and explore their role as active citizens in a democratic society—important activities that are part of these learning exchanges.

Student interns at Weill Cornell Medical College, New York City / Students at a professional development conference in Washington, D.C. with the Cornell Institute for Public Affairs / Molly Warren '10, College of Human Ecology, presents a lesson to fourth-year Kagugu Primary School students in Kigali, Rwanda

Cornell staff and faculty provide engaged learning participants with advice and mentorship, a comprehensive set of strategies, and tools for critical reflection, from group, class, and public presentations to journaling, electronic portfolios, written essays and research reports, and opportunities for publication.

Engaged students at Cornell gain the knowledge, skills, and habits for lifelong learning and active citizenship in our society. Students come together from diverse backgrounds and resources to engage in an honest and critical dialogue on social problems, find common solutions, and act responsibly and collectively to remove these issues from the life of families and communities.

Cornell education for public engagement is about learning how to be a good citizen, how to actively participate in democracy, and, ultimately, how to engage in the practice of "freedom with social responsibility" to transform the world for the betterment of all.

FOR MORE INFORMATION
Cornell Public Service Center: psc.cornell.edu
Engaged Learning + Research: elr.cornell.edu

Sarah Hermes '12

Engaged Learning + Research (EL+R) was a defining feature of my overall experience at Cornell University. As a first-year student, I felt utterly overwhelmed by the numerous, seemingly inaccessible opportunities that Cornell had to offer. I struggled to find my own identity within a sea of so many others and create meaning out of my varied experiences. I serendipitously became connected with Dr. Richard Kiely and EL+R during my junior year. Dr. Kiely provided me access to a network of like-minded students and faculty, and also empowered me to become actively involved in this newfound community. Along with a few other students and the support of both EL+R and the Public Service Center, I helped conceptualize and create The Knitting Club: Connecting Engaged Students. The process of founding this new organization was one of the most profound learning experiences I had while at Cornell. Looking back now as an alum, my greatest hope for the future students of Cornell is that they each find a similar opportunity to feel empowered, connected, supported, and engaged with their community and education. Engaged Learning + Research has both the power and the potential to foster these opportunities and make an incredible difference in the community of Cornell and beyond.

Robin Bigelow '11

In reflecting on my experience at Cornell I realize that the defining moments of my four short years were all related to service learning and community engagement. While I learned about the fundamentals of biology and ethics, my biggest takeaway from my undergraduate experience at Cornell was not what I learned in class but what I learned how to do in service-learning projects.

Freshman year I started working with Partnership for Honduran Health and the non-profit Salud Juntos on a community health program in Honduras. With the executive director, Sheridan Reiger '10, I co-founded and taught an accredited service-learning course, Development of Primary Healthcare in Honduras, in which we prepared other students for a summer of community-based research and public health programming in Honduras. I have been to the same community a total of six times, and have worked with local leaders and collaborators in the United States to establish a better system of clinical and public health. At Cornell I also volunteered and participated in service-learning course work and reflections with REACH at a juvenile detention center, and with a health policy non-profit in the Cornell Urban Scholars Program. These experiences have taught me the importance of collaboration and empowerment in volunteer projects and have given me a sense of responsibility to participate in and work toward a better world. I am now a medical student at Johns Hopkins University.

Eric Woods '11

My service-learning experiences at Cornell dramatically influenced my time while in Ithaca. I gained hands-on experience in social medicine that supplemented the knowledge that I was getting from class. Additionally, I saw first-hand some of the root causes of inequities in modern health care. Meanwhile, I learned about social movements, which helped cement my values and personal ideology. Involvement in programs like Cornell Urban Scholars, Public Service Center Scholars, and the global health minor make up a significant portion of my most cherished memories of my time at school. The things that I gained from my service-learning experiences continue to be important even after graduation. They have helped shape my career trajectory—working to improve the health of under-represented minorities. The relationships that I formed in my service-learning endeavors also helped me find a job quickly when I graduated from college.

Cornell's global programs, research sites, initiatives, and partnerships

Paris, France
- ILR dual degree program with the ESCP-EAP European School of Management
- Paris Summer Institute of International and Comparative Law
- Cornell University Center for Documentation on American Law in Paris

Ontario, Canada
Johnson School Executive MBA program with Queen's School of Business, Kingston

Rome, Italy
AA&P Cornell in Rome program

Mexico
- Latin American Studies Program, Experience Latin America II: Chiapas Edition, field-study course
- Durable Rust Resistance in Wheat project, collaboration with International Maize and Wheat Improvement Center and part of a broad-based global partnership

Spain
Engineering students pilot study-abroad program at University of Cantabria

Dominican Republic
Cornell biodiversity lab and field station at Punta Cana

Elios Proni, Greece
Institute for European Studies fosters sister-city relationship

Port-au-Prince, Haiti
Weill Cornell collaboration with GHESKIO Center on AIDS research

Arecibo, Puerto Rico
Arecibo Observatory, managed by Cornell's National Astronomy and Ionosphere Center for the National Science Foundation

Uganda
Vet College's Expanding Horizons program, mountain gorilla habitat

Honduras
- Civil and environmental engineering's AguaClara Project brings promise of clean, treated water to Ojojona and Támara
- International Veterinary Medicine Abroad program

Ghana
- Cornell's Public Service Center service-learning course in Hujimbre
- Cornell-supported University of Ghana doctoral program

Panama
AA&P's Sustainable Panama, an interdisciplinary winter session workshop course

Nicaragua
- Cornell's chapter of Engineers for a Sustainable World helps Nicaraguan women design and use solar ovens
- Latin American Studies Program, Summer Program in Nicaragua

Colombia
Johnson School professor, Ph.D. student study impact of violence on entrepreneurs, also supported by Einaudi Center travel grant

Rwanda
Institute for African Development and Cornell Law School help draft Rwanda's new code of contract law

Costa Rica
Cornell Wind Ensemble's ongoing music education and outreach project

Tanzania
Weill Cornell physician training and Weill Bugando medical complex

Peru
Cornell's Undergraduate Research Program on Biodiversity's EsBaran Amazon Field Laboratory at Yarapa River Lodge

Zambia
CIIFAD and the Vet College, SANREM in Zambia Partnership with Wildlife Conservation Society to help Community Markets for Conservation

Bolivia
- Vet College's Expanding Horizons program supports students in the field (in several countries)
- Quechua Language Training program

Cerro Chajnantor, Chile
Cornell Caltech Atacama Telescope project

Brazil
Latin American Studies Program's Brazilian Cities Summer Program

South Africa
Cornell's AEM Emerging Markets Program (also in Botswana)

Greater Andes Mountains, Argentina
EAS 4170, Field Camp in the Central Andes, summer course in mapping and geology

Bulgaria
Cornell team helps Bulgaria's University of Rousse develop master's in regional development management

Crete, Greece
Cornell Institute for European Studies fosters partnership for Mediterranean water research

Jordan
Intensive Arabic Program, Department of Near Eastern Studies

Turkey
Cornell Tree-Ring Laboratory Aegean and Near Eastern Dendrochronology Project (also in Israel)

Afghanistan
CIIFAD projects (applied research and development, educational capacity-building, faculty exchange and agroforestry)

Pakistan
The Einaudi Center supports faculty research on Pakistan's contemporary art and popular culture

Nepal
Cornell Nepal Study Program, joint venture with Tribhuvan National University

Beijing, China
- China and Asia-Pacific Studies (CAPS) program
- Cornell Law student exchange program with Peking Law School
- Ongoing partnership with Tsinghua University
- College of Human Ecology collaboration with Peking University exploring how culture shapes personal memories and identities
- East Asia Program partnership with the Inter-University Program for Chinese Language Studies at Qinghua University

Shanghai, China
- The Cornell-China Humanities Institute Initiative, in partnership with three universities
- The Tang Family Cornell-China Scholars Program (multiple sites)

South Korea
- Brain Korea 21, an international collaborative program with Seoul National University
- East Asia Program scholarly exchanges and collaboration with Seoul National University

Japan
- Clarke Program in East Asian Law and Culture research collaboration with the University of Tokyo's Institute of Social Science
- East Asia Program partnership with the Inter-University Center for Japanese Language Studies

Juba, Sudan
Mann Library's Library-in-a-Box makes digital agricultural journals available in Sudan (and 50 other countries)

Doha, Qatar
Weill Cornell Medical College-Qatar

Bangladesh
Student spends eight weeks studying mothers and infants as part of Cornell's new Global Health Program

Hong Kong
Human Ecology's Hong Kong exchange program

Saudi Arabia
Partnership with King Abdullah University of Science and Technology (KAUST)

India
- Joint degree in food science and plant breeding with Tamil Nadu Agricultural University
- International Agriculture and Rural Development 602 field course
- Tata-Cornell Initiative in Agriculture and Nutrition

Philippines
Course at International Rice Research Institute

Ethiopia
- Master of Professional Studies (MPS) degree in international agriculture and rural development with Bahir Dar University

Singapore
Cornell-Nanyang Institute of Hospitality Management, joint Hotel School degree/certificate programs with Nanyang Technological University

Indonesia
Southeast Asia Program and Echols Collection have built a repository of unique materials accessible in Indonesia and 10 other countries comprising the region

Kenya
- CIIFAD Biocomplexity Research project
- Field study with Seeds of Development Program, Cornell
- AEM's Emerging Markets Program Tropical Field Ecology and Behavior (BioEE 2650), three-week summer session course
- Institute for African Development and Cornell Law School reform Kenya's legal infrastructure

Sri Lanka
South Asia Program writes text, records audiovisuals in partnership with the University of Peradeniya for forthcoming Sinhala language textbook

Antanarivo, Madagascar
CIIFAD's System of Rice Intensification

Australia
The Einaudi Center supports graduate student travel for research on Australia's social knowledge systems (one of more than 120 annual travel grants for international graduate studies)

U.S. CAMPUSES
Ithaca, NY Cornell University, Ithaca campus
Geneva, NY New York State Agricultural Experiment Station/College of Agriculture and Life Sciences
New York City, NY Weill Cornell Medical College, Cornell NYC Tech, academic facilities throughout the city
Washington, DC Cornell in Washington Program
Appledore Island, Isle of Shoals, Maine Shoals Marine Laboratory

Locations on map current as of 2009

World map image/istockphoto; illustration and design by Wendy Kenigsberg/Cornell University Communications. Photo (provided by Cornell Abroad)

WAYS TO CONNECT

Explore the winding paths of your imagination and enjoy the scenery along the way. As with any journey, there will be obstacles. These will not be the things that define you. Only you can define you. Cornell is the place for you to do just that.

—Ulysses Smith '13

Above: The Farmers Market at Cornell
Left: Homecoming 2010

Opportunities for Work and Play with the Student Leadership, Engagement, and Campus Activities Office

Catherine Holmes, MS '85, associate dean of students, Cornell University; director, Student Leadership, Engagement, and Campus Activities

Catherine Holmes, associate dean of students, directing the 40-member Krewe during the annual Dragon Day Parade in 2013

"There is no question that student organizations truly enhance the Cornell experience."

Congratulations and welcome to the Cornell community! If you or your student has already visited the Student Leadership, Engagement, and Campus Activities Office (SLECA) website—sleca.cornell.edu—you know that many opportunities await new students who want to get involved. The office coordinates a number of programs and services for the Cornell community, and we look forward to seeing your student in our venues and at programs and events throughout the year. Some of our offerings include:

- Student union and community center programs and services
- Major event registration and consultation
- Student organization registration and accounting support
- Bailey Hall class, event, and technical services
- Part-time employment opportunities for students
- Leadership and student development
- Training, awards, and recognition for clubs and student leaders
- Student union reservations

If your student is looking for a part-time job on campus, encourage him or her to consider applying for a position as a SLECA student staff member. We offer a comprehensive student employment program. Students work in the Willard Straight Hall Resource Center, community centers on North Campus, class councils, the Bailey Hall box office, and with Cornell Productions, a student-managed sound and light company. Students who work with us receive solid training and can advance to leadership positions. Plus, it's fun! Our students

Left: The 2013 Lift Your Spirits student event

constantly interact with people who visit our venues. They also help develop and work at all kinds of events that strive to make their peers feel welcome and connected to the university. Our website has more information about job opportunities.

SLECA's venues include Bailey Hall, Robert Purcell Community Center, Appel Commons, and Willard Straight Hall, the historic student union at Cornell. Bailey Hall is a state-of-the-art performance venue that hosts large academic classes, the Cornell Concert Series, events sponsored by student organizations, and performances by world-class artists. The community centers (Robert Purcell and Appel) welcome new students to North

Class Notes, Cornell's co-ed a cappella group, performs at an event

Campus and offer numerous workshops, programs, and events designed to make them feel connected to the Cornell community. Willard Straight Hall is home to Cornell Cinema, the Office of the Dean of Students, SLECA, the Bear's Den Pub, the Willard Straight Hall Resource Center, and more. We want our students to experience all that these venues have to offer.

There is no question that student organizations truly enhance the Cornell experience. Registered organizations sponsor countless activities and events that may include theatrical performances, movies, concerts, dances, lectures, debates, cultural programs, service in the community, trips off campus,

Cornell's Big Red Band performs on the Ithaca Commons

sporting events, and so much more. Students may choose to sample from these offerings in a number of ways: simply attending a student-organized event is one way to participate, or they can get involved as a member of one or more registered organizations and actively partner with peers to make great things happen on campus. Being a volunteer in a registered organization can help new students meet people with similar interests, learn new skills, gain valuable leadership experience, and make a real difference in the community.

A word of caution: With more than 1,000 registered student organizations at Cornell, and approximately 3,000 major events held on campus each year, it can be very tempting to get "over involved." It's best for first-year students to get settled into their new living space and classes first. Once new students are able to determine just how much of their time they need to devote to academic work, perhaps a part-time job, the balance between study and life, and, of course, sleeping, then we encourage them to jump in and volunteer for an organization and/or engage in some outside pursuits.

If, amid all the wonderful options, students can't find an organization that interests them, they might think about forming a new student organization. First, students should check out our website and make sure there isn't already a registered organization with a similar purpose. The next step is to meet with a SLECA representative to discuss plans and determine what might be needed in order to register. It's fairly simple to register a new organization, and once that is done, it will be eligible to apply for funding through the student activity fee administered by the Undergraduate Student Assembly and the Graduate and Professional Student Assembly and to request permission to use university property for organization-sponsored activities and events.

Jon Stewart, host of the Emmy Award–winning late-night program *The Daily Show*, speaks in Barton Hall during First-Year Parents' Weekend

The Flaming Lips play at Barton Hall

There are two types of student organizations that register with SLECA: independent organizations and university organizations (summarized below). Both provide opportunities for students to volunteer and, with experience, to lead. However, they do provide a different type of experience for those who choose to join. If your student is forming a group or thinking about joining an existing group, it's important to consider how these types of groups might meet their needs.

- Most registered organizations are independent from Cornell University. They are free to form based on current student interest, and they are free to fold when that interest wanes. They must register with SLECA in order to gain access to university facilities and secure a university-affiliated volunteer advisor. Students learn life skills as they undertake the organization's scheduling, financial, legal, and other obligations. Examples include sport clubs (Tennis Club, Sailing Club, etc.), a cappella groups (Nothing But Treble, The Hangovers, etc.), many cultural organizations (Black Students United, Chinese Students and Scholars Association, etc.), and special interest groups (Chess Club, Go Club, Gaming Alliance), and more.

- Approximately one-third of registered groups are university organizations. University organizations exist to support the academic mission of the university and/or the priorities and mission of the campus departments or units in which they are housed. Staff and faculty members advise these organizations as part of their job responsibilities and work closely with them to accomplish the organization's goals. Advisors partner with students to establish the direction of the organization and train members who join throughout the academic year. Examples include college-related groups (Glee Club; Society of Women Engineers; Minority Organization of Arts, Architecture, and Planning; etc.) and most by-line funded organizations (Cornell Concert Commission, Graduate and Professional Students Programming Board, Orientation Steering Committee, etc.).

Before I close, I can't help but put in a shameless plug in hopes that your student will consider joining one of our in-house student organizations. Our experienced staff members work closely with the following groups and we would love to have the opportunity to work with your student. Please visit our website for more details.

- Cornell Concert Commission
- Cornell University Program Board
- CUTonight Funding Commission
- Graduate and Professional Students Programming Board
- North Campus Programming Council
- Senior Convocation Committee
- Senior Week Committee

- Slope Day Programming Board and subcommittees
- Undergraduate Class Councils
- Welcome Weekend
- Willard Straight Hall Student Union Board and subcommittees

The 2012 DJ Power Hour dining event

Finally, please let your student know there are many ways to find out about student organizations and activities happening on campus. Don't underestimate word of mouth, listservs, and social networks! If your student lives on campus, his or her resident advisor can be very helpful. Students can easily browse the student organization directory online. Each fall, more than 3,000 people attend the Welcome Weekend–sponsored ClubFest in Barton Hall, which is an extravaganza that showcases more than 300 registered organizations. (Details for this event can be found in the new student orientation booklet or at rso.cornell.edu/welcomeweekend.) The Cornell Events Calendar is also a great way to find out what's happening on campus: events.cornell.edu.

The Pao Bhangra XII exhibition

Although We're Diverse, Our Similarities Can Bring Us Together

Ulysses Smith '13

Ulysses Smith '13

"The beauty of Cornell is that every student is in the position to bring about meaningful change."

I can still remember the day I opened my acceptance letter to Cornell. I remember the anxiety of holding an envelope that would help to determine the future of my education—an envelope with so much power. After reading those wonderful words of acceptance, the excitement was almost too much to control; however, it soon faded and quickly turned to panic. Now that I had been accepted to an Ivy League institution, I had to figure out what in the world I was going to do. I had to figure out how I was going to make it at a competitive university, which I had neither visited, nor thoroughly researched. This was the beginning of my Cornell experience.

Like most of the other students at Cornell, I came from a competitive high school environment. I did all sorts of extracurricular activities and had pretty good test scores—that part is debatable. The thing that I struggled with when coming to Cornell was how to transfer all of that and apply it to my college experience. When everybody around you is brilliant, competitive, and ambitious, it's not always easy to see how and where you will fit in.

As many people may know, Cornell is a place where people from all walks of life are present. Often times, you will find yourself having lunch in a dining hall surrounded by five separate conversations in five different languages. It is to be expected that you will encounter people from environments and circumstances that you have never been exposed to. I did not live a heavily sheltered life by any means, but I still had never been around so many different people. Being from the South, I grew up aware of the fact that I was from a place that carried the historic stigma of being unaccepting. I was used to being the only person of color in my classes and having to fend off the negative perceptions of black men. It was always my goal to transcend these stereotypes and to become the successful person that I knew I was meant to be.

I have learned here, however, that this is no easy task. I could not begin to tell anyone what I expected to find when I got to Cornell because, truth be told, I really had no clue. I came with six suitcases, on a whim and a prayer. But I can tell you what I found when I got here.

My first week was full of orientation events. I was introduced to what seemed like thousands of new people and added just as many new numbers into my phone. If there is one thing new students will learn during that first week, it's the value that Cornell places on icebreakers—those little games that you are forced to do in order to "break the ice" when meeting new people. I almost thought that I needed to change my name on my birth certificate to add my major and hometown, since that was how I had to introduce myself to every person I encountered. After that week, classes began and reality really set in.

The reality of Cornell was vastly different from the glimpse of the different pockets of campus life you get during orientation week. Just like during my public school education, I found myself being the only person of color in a few of my classes. I found myself in awkward situations when people generalized entire races of people and I felt compelled to explain my own experiences. I found myself floating from different social groups in an effort to find myself, my place, and comfort—all while trying not to limit my experiences.

Kent Hubbell, the Robert W. and Elizabeth C. Staley Dean of Students, with the 2012–2013 Student Assembly

Despite how negative this experience might seem, it really was more positive than I thought at the time. Looking back, I can really appreciate those experiences and how they led me to find ways to make a difference at Cornell.

My experience here at Cornell has been shaped in large part by my involvement in campus governance. I became involved with the Student Assembly (SA) at the beginning of my first year. The SA is the governing body for undergraduate students. I found that through the assembly, I was able to really get involved in the everyday functions of the university. The beauty of Cornell is that every student is in the position to bring about meaningful change. Students are able to learn more about the different policies at the university and even create new ones. Administrators, staff, and faculty make themselves accessible to students so that meaningful dialogues can take place. We handle a plethora of different issues every year that range from the placement of trashcans all the way to anti-discrimination clauses.

Though I have been involved with a number of initiatives, it was only this year that I truly found my passion. Over the course of my semester abroad, I had the opportunity to really reflect on the past few years at Cornell. I was able to examine the issues and circumstances

that I had come across and think about what could have prevented them—how some of these negative experiences could have been positive. This is how I became really focused on the topic of diversity and the various subjects that surround it.

When most people think of diversity, they immediately think of minorities or simply "people of color." It has been my goal to really work with this university to change that thought. The reality is that diversity is a concept that encompasses quite a lot. It's not just about skin color or gender; it's about the various intersections of our identities. Like many other people, I came here being aware of my race. That's not necessarily a bad thing. The problem is that we are not really made aware of the various similarities we have across our identities. Not being aware of those similarities, coupled with not being taught and encouraged to talk across differences, is what inhibited me from really finding my niche early on in my academic career. Cornell has learned much about this very subject and has made incredible strides in addressing it.

Even in what seems to be a chaotic environment sometimes, Cornell gave me something that I know no other place could have provided: a sense of belonging. So my charge to new students is simple: use the time that you are given here to really learn about yourself. You are in a unique position to meet so many new people and go beyond any limits that you might have thought you had. Explore the winding paths of your imagination and enjoy the scenery along the way. As with any journey, there will be obstacles. These will not be the things that define you. Only you can define you. Cornell is the place for you to do just that.

FOR MORE INFORMATION
Student Assembly: assembly.cornell.edu/SA
Diversity and Inclusion: diversity.cornell.edu

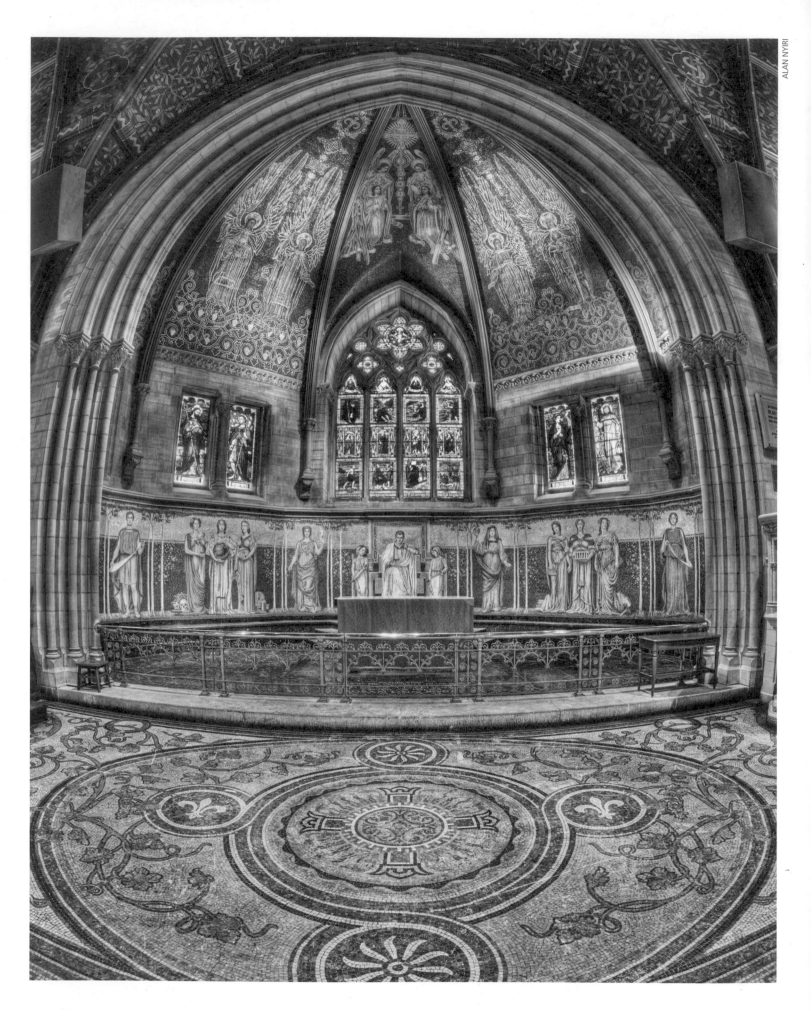

ALAN NYIRI

Religion and Spiritual Life at Cornell

Ken Clarke, associate dean of students, Cornell University; director, Cornell United Religious Work

Ken Clarke

"Cornell United Religious Work stands at the ready to assist students in their religious and spiritual journeys."

Cornell has long prided itself as an institution where "any person can find instruction in any study." These words of founder Ezra Cornell, which are the university's motto, reflect a democratic accessibility and openness to persons of diverse backgrounds, identities, experiences, and creeds. Further, the university's decision to establish itself as a nonsectarian institution unaffiliated with any mainline Protestant denomination (which led to severe criticism in some quarters within mid-nineteenth-century higher education and religious communities) laid the groundwork not only for diversity of ideas but, ultimately, diversity of religious communities at Cornell.

Cornell United Religious Work (CURW) represents such religious diversity. Emanating from its nineteenth-century roots as the Cornell University Christian Association, CURW became the first intentionally multifaith organization on a major U.S. campus in 1929. By 1934 it included Jews, Protestants, Roman Catholics, Unitarians, and Quakers. The presence of a multifaith organization on a campus such as Cornell was not insignificant. This was a historical moment at a time when the religious, cultural, political, and economic dominance of mainline Protestantism as *de facto* American religion remained powerful. And the majority of similar campuses were years,

Buddhist monks from the Namgyal Monastery lead prayers on the Arts Quad

if not decades, away from incorporating such a multifaith model. Hence, CURW's founding was, in symbol and substance, reflective of an institution that from its inception had been characterized by admirers and critics for "thinking otherwise."

Today's CURW is composed of 29 religious and spiritual organizations representative of a contemporary American religious landscape that has become increasingly diverse during the last 50 years. Since 1934, the aforementioned faith communities have been joined by Muslims, Zen Buddhists, Tibetan Buddhists, evangelical Christians, Hindus, and those attending African American worship services. A number of these groups are served and supported by chaplains (CURW affiliate staff) employed by their faith communities whose relation to the university is through membership in CURW.

Left: Sage Chapel

JANELLE HANSON

Cornell United Religious Work: Fostering interfaith community since 1929

Our chaplain colleagues report to the boards, dioceses, parachurch organizations, churches, and other authoritative entities of their respective communities. Other groups are student-led organizations advised by faculty or staff. CURW-member groups provide opportunities for worship, study of sacred texts, community service, alternative spring break activities, and various forms of mission work and educational activities that sometimes involve international travel. All of these activities are intended to contribute to the spiritual, intellectual, emotional, and psychological expansion—or holistic development—of students.

My hope is that students involved in CURW will be well-educated contributors to society and the world, motivated by values representing the highest ideals of their faith traditions, respectful of the right of others to adhere to beliefs different from their own, and supporters of the advancement of civic good and community by finding common ground with others.

CURW's administrative office (CURW core staff) is responsible for the administration, coordination, and facilitation of religious affairs on campus. CURW is also the administrative office for Anabel Taylor Hall (the campus multifaith center and last of the Collegiate Gothic buildings erected at Cornell) and Sage Chapel (one of Cornell's most beloved and architecturally attractive buildings). CURW is one of the offices that reports to the dean of students and is part of the Division of Student and Academic Services.

A core value of CURW is the belief that religion has a contribution to make to the educational mission and intellectual life of the university. Toward that end, CURW sponsors several programs during the academic year that explore innovative religious thought (Frederick C. Wood Lecture) and the intersection between science, religion, and society (Robert W. and Mabel D. Beggs Lecture). It also hosts campus and community speakers who discuss their motivation and hope in their work and lives, often in relation to social justice (Soup and Hope), provides alumni in the New York City region opportunities for intellectual stimulation (CURW in the City), and invites the

campus community to reflect on the legacy of one of the greatest global exemplars of spirit, intellect, and social justice (Martin Luther King, Jr. Commemoration).

In fact, the motto for Sage Chapel, used for worship services, lectures, and concerts, is "Where Spirit and Intellect Meet." Some of the most notable preachers, religious leaders, theologians, scholars, journalists, and cultural critics of the twentieth and twenty-first centuries have spoken at the chapel, including Dr. King, Abraham Joshua Heschel, Karen Armstrong, Carl Sagan, Arianna Huffington, Amy Goodman, Eboo Patel, and Cornel West. It is the primary university location for quiet personal reflection and meditation, occasions of joyous expectation (weddings), and solemn, yet at times celebratory, remembrances (memorial services).

Meanwhile, Anabel Taylor bustles with activity of the faith communities and broader university events on any given day of the academic year, especially in the evenings. Many of CURW's groups meet and are headquartered here, while others meet elsewhere on campus. This building also houses a new baroque organ, built with baroque period implements, which is based on the plans of a renowned eighteenth-century Schnitger organ in the Charlottenburg Palace, Berlin, destroyed in the Allied bombings of World War II. In the vestibule leading to the organ's location in Anabel Taylor Chapel is a small meditation room, yet another opportunity for students and others to experience a break from the frenetic pace of Cornell life.

I acknowledge that the college years are a time of intellectual expansion as well as exploration and experimentation with spiritual, social, cultural, and political options previously not considered. This expansion, exploration, and experimentation is culturally conditioned by the time in which we live at any given moment. This moment in the twenty-first century is one of dramatic cultural and technological shifts. College student development scholar Arthur W. Levine, in an address at Sage Chapel, outlined these shifts:

• The pervasive instability or collapse of nuclear families

- The testimony of many young adults that they have never witnessed a successful romantic relationship among older adults

- Distrust of social institutions such as government and churches, regardless of ideological leanings

- The sense among young people that they inherited, from their parents' generations, massive social and political problems that they cannot ignore

- The launching of lone individuals into cyberspace by way of their computers

- An all-encompassing consumer culture offering an endless stream of products

These factors have influenced a wandering, seeker type of spirituality among students who often describe themselves as being "spiritual but not religious." Being spiritual connotes being on a quest, a journey, something not yet completed, whereas for many students "religion" means something fixed, completed, handed down. The journey of spiritual student development is at times a road replete with potholes, troublesome turns, and detours.

Students in pursuit of spiritual connection may find themselves wrestling with a faith as they experienced it prior to college, exposure to different interpretations of their faith tradition, or attraction to another faith or belief system altogether. Once they are confronted with a personal crisis, some students undergo a crisis of faith, a period of doubt and questioning as they reexamine their spiritual and theological assumptions. These personal crises may include the death of a loved one, an unplanned pregnancy, divorce of one's parents, or coming to terms with an emergent sexual identity.

"In all our work, CURW hopes to foster a spirit of welcome, inclusion, respect, and hospitality."

Internal wrestling is normal. Such an experience, at its best, can lead to a much richer, fuller comprehension and practice of one's faith. Conversely, some students experience a profound disorientation that can be cause for concern. As a parent you may notice:

- Students becoming more absolutist in their assertions, especially in discussing how class subject matter intersects with faith/ spiritual issues

- Previously engaged students becoming disinterested in classroom participation and assignments

- Withdrawal

- The report of oppositional behavior in the classroom or in interactions with others; you may experience such opposition directly

Cornell United Religious Work stands at the ready to assist students in their religious and spiritual journeys. As director, I am available for pastoral counseling, as are our associate director and CURW chaplains who represent diverse faith traditions. In instances in which a student's psychological and religious concerns are related, CURW can work in concert with Cornell's Counseling and Psychological Services to provide support. We welcome students, as well as faculty or staff, of any or no religious affiliation.

This welcome to all symbolizes the intent of the donor who provided the funding for the construction of our multifaith center, Anabel Taylor Hall. It was Myron Taylor (1874–1959), an 1894 Cornell Law School graduate who was a leading U.S. industrialist and first ambassador to the Vatican. Mr. Taylor named the building to honor his wife and established its location adjacent to the Law School building named for him. At the dedication of Anabel Taylor Hall in October 1952, he spoke of his hopes for the building:

" . . . Here is one place where all religions may repair for worship and for that inward reflection upon God and immortality, which precede and follow sincere worship, however voiced. Here a lonely soul may meditate and pray by himself; here, groups may gather; here, a numerous congregation may join in songs of praise. If rules be necessary for the governance of this sanctuary, let them be such as promote tolerance and a quiet respect for religious ideas and customs not our own. Here, majority opinion need not rule, to the confusion of the individuals; neither shall a minority stir tumult in the hearts of others."

Sixty-one years later, a cohort of students carries on the vision of Myron Taylor through efforts to promote interfaith dialogue, which include organizing dinners and other events. Sixty-one years hence, a partnership between CURW, Cornell Hillel, and Interfaith Youth Core of Chicago, seeks to promote a climate of cooperation among students of diverse faiths and philosophies of life through student support and partnerships with students and academic offices across campus. Sixty-one years afterward, proactive efforts are being pursued to invoke deeper levels of understanding and interaction within our diverse community of chaplains. This is the continuity of work that began more than eight decades ago in the effort to foster multifaith and interfaith community.

In all our work, CURW hopes to foster a spirit of welcome, inclusion, respect, and hospitality. We welcome our students to visit our buildings, learn about our programs and faith communities, and make choices to engage based on their individual consciences. We hope they will experience the spirit we seek daily to foster.

FOR MORE INFORMATION
Cornell United Religious Work: curw.cornell.edu

Greek Life at Cornell

Travis Apgar, the Robert G. Engel Associate Dean of Students, Office of Fraternities, Sororities, and Independent Living

Travis Apgar

"There is no doubt the Cornell fraternity and sorority experience can have a lasting, positive effect on members."

In founding this esteemed university in 1865, Ezra Cornell and Andrew Dickson White began with the idea that Cornell would not be a residential campus. Rather, students would live amongst Ithacans and their families. However, it did not take long (1868), for Cornellians to think otherwise and create student housing in the form of fraternities and, later, sororities. This decision fulfilled some basic needs for students, as it provided a place to lay one's head, to study, to live. It also fulfilled higher-level student needs, such as having an association with a social network and receiving emotional support. These groups regularly transcend the standard perceptions and provide a place to live and/or socialize. At Cornell, most fraternities and sororities offer housing, and while the house may be referred to as home away from home, the groups develop a unique bond that is somehow more than friendship, regardless of the presence of a physical structure. This powerful bond is reflected in the words used to describe fellow members: brothers and sisters. This bond of membership is developed around a set of similar ideals, values, experiences, and interests that make the relationship closer in comparison to that of a family. This

The 2011 Greek Leaders Retreat

experience provides student members not only a home away from home, but also a family away from family. Yet, there's more.

Social fraternities and sororities exist on nearly 1,000 college campuses in the United States and are too often misunderstood, as societal perspectives are formed through the lens of the popular media, which typically portrays the experience as a cycle of alcohol abuse,

Left: Interior of the Chi Psi fraternity house at 810 University Avenue

Cornell Outdoor Education leadership training 2013 with Sigma Nu and Delta Gamma

TODD MINER

hazing, and other assorted debauchery. While there is no doubt that behavioral challenges exist, this limited perspective fails to inform those who are unfamiliar with the desirable benefits that membership offers. As a community, Cornell remains committed to eradicating practices that endanger the health and well-being of our students. The university has recently refocused its approach to addressing high-risk behaviors in order to identify innovative methods that will produce the desired culture changes. Greek letter organizations at Cornell have played a significant role in the student living-learning experience outside of the classroom. They have persisted, despite the challenges, because of the value they offer. We recognize this experience as worthwhile and believe that it will continue to have a place on this campus and within this community. It is with that in mind that we aim to preserve all that is positive and good about the experience as we support our student leaders and alumni through this period of evolution.

The Chi Psi fraternity house at 810 University Avenue

Collegiate Greek-letter organizations can trace their roots back to 1776 (the era of the American Revolution) and the establishment of a secret society called Phi Beta Kappa. Five students at the College of William and Mary established this secret society to give their peers the opportunity to come together to discuss contemporary topics and matters, which was something the faculty members of that time were opposed to. Today, Phi Beta Kappa is a highly regarded academic honor society. In similar fashion, fraternities and sororities have been established all over the country with various intents and purposes. Cornell is a campus of great significance among the national fraternal community, as it served as birthplace for five distinguished national fraternities and sororities. The organizations

that were founded here are the Alpha Phi Alpha Fraternity, Inc., the first intercollegiate Greek-letter fraternity established for African Americans (1906); Delta Chi Fraternity, Inc., initially formed with an academic focus

The Alpha Phi Alpha Fraternity Inc. silent march down Campus Road to celebrate its centennial

on law (1890); Sigma Delta Tau Sorority, established by women who had experienced religious discrimination by other sororities of the time (1917); La Unidad Latina, Lambda Upsilon Lambda Fraternity, Inc., a fraternal service organization aimed at uniting men in brotherhood in order to serve the Latino community (1982); and Latinas Promoviendo Comunidad, Lambda Pi Chi Sorority, Inc., the first Latina-focused sorority founded at an Ivy League institution (1988). Over the generations, our Greek community has metaphorically scaled down Cornell's sizable campus and student body, providing students an opportunity for camaraderie with peers of a particular background or with like interests as they broaden their own experiences and appreciation for difference.

Today's Cornell Greek community is one of the largest in the country, boasting more than 60 fraternities and sororities and more than 4,200 student members, approximately one-third of the undergraduate student population. While these organizations are recognized and granted benefits by the university, they are independent entities that make up a self-governing community. Each chapter belongs to one of three councils: the Interfraternity Council, the Panhellenic Council, or the Multicultural Greek Letter Council. The Office for Fraternities, Sororities, and Independent Living provides support, guidance,

The 2012 Greek Leaders Retreat

Greeks helping new students move in on Opening Day

Victory Club, an annual black-tie charity ball sponsored by Alpha Delta Phi fraternity, has helped to raise tens of thousands of dollars for local charities. In 2013, ADP raised more than $11,000 for the Ithaca Public Education Initiative.

advocacy, and advisement to all groups, councils, and students within this community. The three governing councils consist of students who have been elected by their peers to serve in officer positions for one-year terms. These student leaders create opportunities for organizational success through educational programs, service opportunities, and civic engagement. They also develop and enforce community standards and expectations. There are a wide variety of developmental experiences available to those who choose to join, which often provide students with valuable life skills.

Each year, members of fraternities and sororities contribute tens of thousands of hours to service and advocacy on campus, in the greater Ithaca area, and around the world. They also raise hundreds of thousands of dollars for worthy causes, such as charities and research. These activities are not compelled. There are no requirements for chapters to engage in service or philanthropic endeavors. They do it because it is at the core of each of these organization's values to better the community around them and the people who are members. Service activities lend to both of those goals. Cornell students who belong to a fraternity or sorority, compared to those who do not, are more likely to contribute to the community. Members report outgaining their non-member peers in interpersonal skills, such as written and oral communication, leadership, functioning on a team, and resolving conflict. They also report being well prepared for their careers. In fact, more than 90 percent of students who belong to a fraternity or sorority rated their educational experience at Cornell as "excellent" or "good," a higher rating than that from their peers who are not fraternity or sorority members.

One need only spend time with a Cornellian who was active in his or her fraternity or sorority to understand the tangible benefits they offer, many of which are considered critical to students' life successes. I regularly have the privilege of meeting Cornellians who have achieved amazing goals in their lives and careers. These wonderful people have

positively contributed to our national and global communities in roles as responsible government and corporate leaders, educators, scientists, medical professionals, philanthropists, writers, and inventors. One of the first alums I met with in beginning my work here at Cornell was the CEO of one of the world's largest and most successful corporations. I was astonished as I listened to this person's lessons learned and the description of the chapter steward and a member of a governing council who were primary building blocks in this leader's professional development. It made clear to me how impactful this experience could be. Yet, there's more.

There is no doubt the Cornell fraternity and sorority experience can have a lasting, positive effect on members. But we also know there are challenges associated with the American college experience pertaining to risky behaviors, often involving alcohol, and other associated behaviors that frequently accompany over-consumption. Students in the Cornell community are not immune. They, like their peers on other campuses, are faced with difficult social choices. They arrive on campus trying to identify their new social network. They are posed with many choices early on that have to do with consuming alcohol or other drugs, or not. Should they participate in hazing activities? What about sexual relationships? I could go on. We are committed, as a community, to addressing activities that are incongruent with the mission of our institution. In particular, actions that create an unsafe physical or emotional environment, disrupt students' scholarly endeavors, or are antithetical to our commitment to diversity and inclusion.

We have spent the past two years following President Skorton's challenge to "end pledging as we know it" by addressing the risky activities incongruent with the core principles and values of the fraternity and sorority experience and by engaging with students, alumni, faculty, national fraternity and sorority representatives, and other topic experts to reformulate our approaches specific to the prevention of hazing, alcohol and drug abuse, sexual misconduct, and other bias-related offenses.

Perhaps the most palpable example of this work is the shift from a pledge model of new member initiation to a model of ongoing membership development, which is free from any form of hazing and ever-focused on the betterment of members through appropriate activities. Those who choose to join a fraternity or sorority now engage with the organization during a four-week orientation period in which the group shares critical information about membership and spends time building bonds among the brotherhood or sisterhood. This provides the new member a critical opportunity to decide if they have chosen the right group for them. Unlike joining most other student organizations, membership in a fraternity or sorority offers a lifelong benefit. While the experience may often focus on the undergraduate portion, bonds among alumni last a lifetime.

We have seen success. We know that some of the changes to and enforcement of policies have made a difference. We know that redefining the new member initiation process has resulted in a reduction of hazing activities. Progress is being made. Having stated that, there remains room for improvement. Specifically, students need support and guidance from their families. The relationship you have with your student is most influential, even if it doesn't always seem so.

We are often asked: What can families do to help? The general answer is to be supportive and help your student think through each decision by considering the consequences and rewards in a realistic manner. Students often have a skewed, unrealistic perspective of how relationship decisions made today will impact their lifelong social status.

The best way to support your student is to have a solid understanding of the issues and the campus resources available to address problematic activities. Resources to familiarize yourself with:

- **hazing.cornell.edu** has perhaps the most comprehensive collection of information related to hazing. It explains what constitutes hazing, why it occurs, prevalence data, and ideas for alternatives to hazing. Most importantly, this web page provides community members with a confidential reporting mechanism if hazing occurs, or is about to occur, so that we can intervene to prevent mental or physical harm.

- **greeks.cornell.edu** offers additional information for students and families to become better acquainted with the fraternity and sorority community at Cornell. With more than 60 organizations for students to consider, we strongly advise that families and students familiarize themselves with as many groups as possible before settling on any small number of groups, so that the best match can be made. You can also find updates on the community's work to address issues of risk while promoting positive activities for student engagement.

Having worked with students and families for years, I know there are plenty of opportunities for family to support their student during his or her college experience. One time in particular is during the fraternity and sorority recruitment period. At Cornell, most students join in the second semester of their first year, but the number who join during the first semester of their sophomore year is increasing.

> "Encourage your student to ask the tough questions—it will give him or her baseline information to help in making the decision about which chapter is best."

Recruitment, sometimes referred to as Rush, can be complicated and stressful for those who desire to join as they navigate these organizations' social networks and pursue those that best fit them. By being familiar with the process, you can provide them with good direction and advice. The best advice is for them to ask for help if they need insight or have questions. As a family member, here are questions you will want your student to consider as he or she enters the process:

- What kinds of service and philanthropy activities (or civic interests) is the chapter and/or its members involved in?

- How much are dues, room and board, and other costs?

- If the fraternity or sorority has a house, are there live-in requirements, and if so, what are they?

- What is new member orientation/initiation like? Is it time consuming? What activities will you engage in to get to know one another? What other requirements are involved?

- What are the benefits of membership, socially and beyond?

- How might you become involved in leadership opportunities?

While some of these are innocuous questions, others are more difficult to ask. Encourage your student to ask the tough questions—it will give him or her baseline information to help in making the decision about which chapter is best.

Please know, and be sure your student knows, that this process is about mutual selection. If the chapter, an independent organization, thinks your student is a good fit, and your student agrees, then an offer, or "bid," for membership will be extended. The vast majority of students with an interest in becoming a member do join. Each year, however, there are students who do not receive an invitation to the organization they had first hoped, which can be disappointing. If they enter the process with an open mind toward all the organizations and give different groups an honest chance, they will find a group that they will fit with, a group they will consider some of their closest friends for the rest of their lives. When your son or daughter is facing this kind of social and personal adversity, your role as a supportive, nurturing parent is critical. Encourage him or her to have an open mind and to explore all the options. If he or she decides to join his or her second- or third-choice fraternity or sorority or one of the nearly 1,000 other student organizations at Cornell, your son or daughter will develop great friendships, a support network, and a social community—and he or she will still have an excellent college experience.

I will leave you with this: Take advantage of all of the resources this dynamic and caring community has to offer you and your student. As a campus community our goal is to provide your student with an excellent and safe collegiate experience so he or she can leave Cornell equipped with tools needed to be successful in whatever path he or she takes in life. There will be challenges along the way, in and out of the classroom. You wouldn't want it otherwise. But, when he or she needs support, together we must be there to provide a caring ear, reassurance, guidance, and advice for how to resolve the challenge.

Please do not hesitate to reach out to our office should you have additional questions. Also see the "Living in the Community" chapter of this book.

FOR MORE INFORMATION
Greek life: greeks.cornell.edu

In Athletics and Academics, Perseverance is Key

Julie Platt Farlow '97, associate head coach, Cornell women's softball

Julie Platt Farlow '97

"Our players love calling home to tell mom and dad they went 3 for 3 in the game with two doubles and a home run. Equally important, though much more difficult, is the call when they go 0 for 3 with three strikeouts and an error."

The leap from high school to collegiate athletics is enormous. Athletes are bigger, stronger, faster, more refined, more experienced, and more knowledgeable. For young first-year students, this is eye opening. They wonder how they will ever catch up. How will they be ready for the next level of competition? Spending time in the weight room and on the practice field is a start. But success doesn't just happen. It demands a commitment by each athlete and a willingness to break down her mechanics, accept change, and rebuild. Skills that were adequate at the high school level may need to be improved. Routines and levels of effort that were once acceptable may need to be intensified. Simply put, what worked in the past may no longer be sufficient.

For us, the successful athlete is one who recognizes her potential for growth and development. She acknowledges her weaknesses and is willing to take the necessary steps to improve them. She can accept constructive criticism and is open to suggestions. She'll ask for help. This is no easy task. Someone who has had athletic success—enough to advance to the Division I level—certainly wants to continue on that path. But as the competition gets stronger she, too, must get better. Inevitably, there will be bumps in the road. How our athletes respond to these obstacles is one of the most important experiences of their early college years.

When a pitcher struggles throwing her curve ball for a strike, she can't simply eliminate that pitch from her repertoire. She must extend beyond her comfort zone and seek help. She must use the available resources to improve her skills and better her performance. What was once mindlessly simple might now be a challenge. If instant success isn't found, she must be patient and continue her efforts.

The same is true academically. Every student at Cornell found success in high school. Their success was rewarded with admission to this fine Ivy League institution. However, as is the case in athletics, more will be demanded of them at the college level. How will they respond when they encounter difficulties? The successful students will recognize their struggles and evaluate their skill sets, their efforts, and their abilities with an open mind. They will be willing to seek help. Again, this is no easy task, especially if academic success was easily achieved at the high school level. The successful students will recognize and be willing to use available resources. The successful students will be patient.

As parents, often miles and miles away, your support is critical. Our players love calling home to tell mom and dad they went 3 for 3 in the game with two doubles and a home run. Equally important, though much more difficult, is the call when they go 0 for 3 with three strikeouts and an error. There will be letdowns. There might be the poor grade in math shortly after the euphoric A- in chemistry.

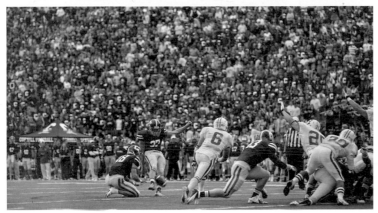

With each passing day, our players develop a maturity to quickly handle setbacks and continue on. As infants learning to walk, we took three steps forward and then fell down. Sometimes we even cried. As toddlers, we advanced from a tricycle to training wheels to a two-wheeler. Again, there were times we fell down and even cried. Success wasn't instantaneous. But with continued effort and patience the goal was achieved. As parents, let your child trip. Let her or him stumble. Let your student fall down and even let him or her cry. But be a pillar of support and a shoulder to lean on. Guide your student with encouragement and reason. Because with continued efforts, with patience, and with help . . . success can be achieved.

Physical Education at Cornell

J. Andrew Noel, the Meakem◆Smith Director of Athletics and Physical Education

J. Andrew Noel

As director of both physical education and recreational services, I have the absolute best job on the Cornell campus. (Well, prior to this job I had the two other best jobs on campus as head coach of the women's volleyball team, and then director of intramural sports.) It's my responsibility to provide fun and healthy activities for Cornell students and staff when they are not in their academic classes or at work. What could be a better job than creating fun all day?! For many years the Cornell Faculty Senate has deemed that it is important for students to have a well-rounded education, which includes taking care of their well-being and their minds. Thus all incoming first-year students have a two-credit physical education requirement. The Department of Physical Education offers more than 250 different classes each semester to help students fulfill this requirement. Greater than 35 percent of our enrollees are students who have already completed their two required classes and are just taking more for their own enjoyment and well-being. Since Cornell faculty, staff, and graduate students are also permitted to take our physical education classes, our undergraduates have a unique opportunity to interact with their professors and their TAs in a completely different setting.

Cornell University encourages its undergraduate students to use their four years here to expand their horizons, try new things, meet new people, get outside of their comfort zones, and take charge of their physical and mental health. The Cornell physical education program provides a great avenue for students to do so.

FOR MORE INFORMATION
Cornell University Wellness Program: wellness.cornell.edu
Cornell Intramural Sports: intramurals.athletics.cornell.edu
Cornell University Physical Education: pe.cornell.edu

Cornell's LGBT Resource Center

Matthew Carcella, associate dean of students, Cornell University; director, LGBT Resource Center

Matthew Carcella

"We serve not only students who identify as LGBTQ, but also our allies, in creating a campus and community that is equitable in every respect."

In the spring of 1968, a group of Cornell students founded the nation's second student organization for lesbian, gay, bisexual, and transgender students. The Cornell Student Homophile League was the start of Cornell's recognition and support for LGBT students, staff, and faculty on campus. Today, the LGBT Resource Center serves as the central hub of LGBTQ life on campus. (The "Q" is included to represent "queer," an increasingly used identity among young adults.) Our mission is to coordinate the efforts of the entire Cornell University community to ensure the inclusion of all lesbian, gay, bisexual, and transgender people and to eliminate heterosexism and gender identity oppression on campus. We are a strong and vibrant community that provides services to faculty and staff, and boasts more than 20 LGBT-specific organizations for undergraduate, graduate, and professional students.

Founded in 1994, the LGBT Resource Center is housed at 626 Thurston Avenue on North Campus. We offer a broad range of educational, support, and social programming to our campus community of nearly 30,000. We serve not only students who identify

A rally on Ho Plaza to support the lesbian, gay, bisexual, and transgender (LGBT) community at Cornell and in Ithaca

as LGBTQ, but also our allies, in creating a campus and community that is equitable in every respect. Student support and engagement is at the heart of what we do. As the overall climate for LGBTQ people has improved in the United States over the past two decades, we see an increasing number of students who are already out (a figure of speech for lesbian, gay, bisexual, and transgender people's disclosure of their sexual orientation and/or gender identity) when they come to

Left: Know the Power of Your Words; a student-sponsored discussion on the implications of bias and bigotry

campus. However, those questioning or struggling with their sexual orientation or gender identity have access to some of the best programs and services in the nation through the LGBT Resource Center.

Students can come to the LGBT Resource Center to talk with staff about coming out, and peer mentors are available for anonymous conversations every evening from 9 to 11 p.m. via our online chat system, faQ Online (lgbtrc.cornell.edu/dos/cms/lgbt/faqchatlogin.cfm).

In addition to the LGBT Resource Center's groups, programs, and services, we also work closely with our academic partners: the LGBT studies program and the Human Sexuality Collection (HSC). The LGBT studies program is housed within the College of Arts and Sciences. Undergraduate and graduate students can opt to complete a minor in LGBT studies through a variety of courses offered in various schools and colleges each semester. Our Human Sexuality Collection, located in the Kroch Library, is part of the Division of

Rare and Manuscript Collections. Founded in 1988, the HSC is one of the oldest and largest collections of human sexuality material in the country. Cornellians are also part of many of the nation's leading LGBT civil rights organizations.

We are proud to be a leader in LGBTQ support services in higher education. Cornell strongly believes in promoting a campus climate that enables all students to succeed, regardless of identity. Feel free to visit our website to learn more, and never hesitate to email us with questions or concerns or for additional resources at lgbtrc@cornell.edu.

FOR MORE INFORMATION
LGBT Resource Center: lgbtrc.cornell.edu
LGBT Studies Program: www.arts.cornell.edu/lgbt

Top (left to right): New students enjoy Bingo Night in Willard Straight Hall, sponsored by the Lesbian, Gay, Bisexual and Transgender (LGBT) Resource Center / Know the Power of Your Words; a discussion on the implications of bias and bigotry / Cornell has an active LGBT alumni organization that sponsors events and socials in cities around the country, particularly New York City, Los Angeles, San Francisco, Washington, and Miami / Dan Savage, syndicated sex columnist, speaks about the It Gets Better project to reach out to LGBT youth who are dealing with their newly discovered sexuality / Students listen to "LGBT Rights and the Supreme Court: Issues and Analysis" with Professor Michael Dorf and Arthur Eisenberg '68, legal director of the New York Civil Liberties Union

"It Gets Better" for Parents, Too

Dale Bernstein '76, founder and principal, UnCommon Human Resources;
vice chair, Diversity Committee, President's Council of Cornell Women

Dale Bernstein '76

"The most important thing my husband and I said to our son that night is that we love him, no matter what. This is what your child needs to hear from you, even if you are struggling with this new information."

Our son "came out" to us in the spring of his first year in college. And even though part of me already knew this (strictly through mom's intuition), and even though we are a family that has cherished gay family and friends, the news hit me right in my gut. I am a mom and a worrier by nature. So questions and fears began to fill my head. Would he be safe? Stories like Matthew Sheppard's certainly put a parent of a gay child on edge. Would his life now be harder? Would his career options be more limited? What if he needed or wanted to move to a less gay-friendly state? Would he find love, be able to get married, have children? (And yes, he will remind me that one of the things I said to him the night he came out was that he was most decidedly not relieved of the duty to provide grandchildren—eventually.)

But the most important thing my husband and I said to our son that night is that we love him, no matter what. This is what your child needs to hear from you, even if you are struggling with this new information. By the time your child tells you she or he is gay, they have likely wrestled for a long time to figure it out and to begin to share. Their concerns may parallel yours and may well be compounded with fears that they will not be accepted—by you, by other family and friends, even by society. They trust you to know this very important part of them, and reassurance (even if you are not ready for acceptance) is what they need.

The average age a person comes out (defined as the act of telling others that one is gay) is now in the mid to late teens. Various reports place the percent of the population that is gay at 4.5 to 10 percent. Seven out of 10 Americans say they know someone who is gay. The college years are a very likely time for you to hear your child is gay, or you may be asked to be there as support for one of his or her friends.

So, where do you turn if you need help? Here at Cornell, there are student organizations, guidance teams, professors, other students, and the Lesbian, Gay, Bisexual, Transgender (LGBT) Resource Center. I always send parents first to PFLAG (Parents, Families, and Friends of Lesbians and Gays)—the nation's foremost family-based organization committed to the civil rights of LGBT people. For full disclosure, I think so highly of

this organization that I serve on its national board of directors. PFLAG, founded 40 years ago by Jeanne Manford—a mom who simply wanted to support her gay son—has grown into an organization with more than 200,000 members. They are parents just like you who are looking for information, answers, and support. With 250 local chapters in every state, chances are there is a PFLAG group near where you live. The website, pflag.org, contains links to information and a tremendous number of resources for you and for your child.

Some key points to keep in mind:

Every reaction is different and valid. You and your significant other may even react differently. Get information. Re-group. Keep the dialogue open with your child. Your child is still the same person that he or she was before coming out to you.

This is a process. Remember that your son or daughter had plenty of time to think about his or her identity before sharing. Don't be hard on yourself if you need some time to get used to this new world.

You are not alone. There are more than eight million self-identified LGBT people in the United States, and they all have families. Talk to others. Seek help.

You are on a journey. And like any journey, there may be good days and bad. ". . . Know that many families before you have taken this same path and have arrived in a place they feel is better than where they started—closer to their children, closer to their families, and closer to an entire community that they never knew existed." (Source, in part, from "Our Daughters and Sons," which can be found here: *pflag.org/freepublications*.)

And now, 10 years later, how am I doing with my original concerns? My son has a successful, challenging career in a field not necessarily thought of as gay friendly. He is happy, in love, and about to get married. And yes, they both want children. It really does get better!

LIVING IN THE COMMUNITY

We often speak of "living and learning" or the "out-of-class experience." Regardless of what we call it, the underlying commitment remains the same: an obligation to the development of the whole student.

—Joseph Burke, PhD

Above: Scenes from the South Asia Shaadi, organized by the Society for India, Pakistani Student Association, and the Bengali Student Association

Left: Students move into North Campus residence halls during Move-In Day 2012

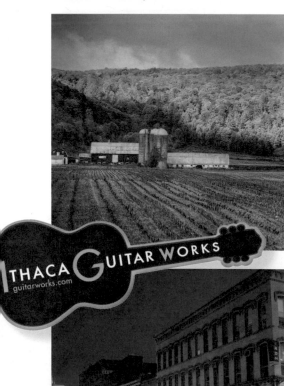

THINGS TO DO AND SEE IN
ITHACA

ITHACA'S DISCOVERY TRAIL is a partnership of top attractions: the kid-friendly Sciencenter, the world-famous Cornell Lab of Ornithology, the wild animals of the Cayuga Nature Center, the botanic gardens of Cornell Plantations, the amazing fossil specimens at the Museum of the Earth, the art collections at Cornell's Herbert F. Johnson Museum of Art, the local artifacts at the History Center, and timely cultural events at the Tompkins County Public Library / **TAKE A HIKE** at Taughannock Falls State Park; Taughannock Falls carves a 400-foot-deep gorge through layers of sandstone, shale, and limestone, once the bed of an ancient sea; with a 215-foot plunge, this waterfall stands three stories taller than Niagara Falls (photo by Tom Schwabel, ENG '99) / **SAVOR A MEAL** at the famous Moosewood Restaurant ("40 Years and still cooking!") or at any of the area's fine eateries / Enjoy a Finger Lakes **WINE-TASTING EXPERIENCE** on the Cayuga Lake Wine Trail; "See It! Taste It! Live It! Love It!" (photo by Brad Phillips) / Visit the **WIDE AWAKE BAKERY**, which uses locally grown grain and flour; located in Mecklenburg, just a few miles from Ithaca (art by Q. Cassatti) / **ITHACA ART TRAIL** features 46 studios and 47 artists; Ithaca and Tompkins

County is packed with talent, visit our artists and see art where it happens (featured fiber artist Sally Dutko's "Sixty-Four") / **VISIT A FARM** in Tompkins County; of the 100,000 acres of farmland owned or operated in the county, approximately 60,000 acres are active, and of that, 16,000 acres are organically managed (photo by Vikas Garg) / **DINE** at Northstar: "Great food, lively libations, and nice, nice vibes" (photo by Andrew Noyes) / **MEET A CRAFTSMAN** like Jonathan Kline, a basket-maker in Trumansburg, who handcrafts black-ash baskets that remain true to function and native materials (photo by Andrew Gillis) / **STROLL** on the Ithaca Commons; experience the remaking of our center city as a re-build project is underway (photo by Shannon Williamson) / **GIMME COFFEE** is, according to the *New York Times*, ". . . obsessed with each detail from farm to cup" (photo by Robert Barker) / **TAKE A CRUISE** and enjoy a daily lunch, brunch, cocktail, or dinner cruise aboard the *M/V Columbia* on scenic Cayuga Lake (photo by Mark H. Anbinder '89) / **CATCH A SHOW** at the State Theatre of Ithaca, which hosts more than 75 events each year, including concerts, theatrical productions, comedy shows, dance performances, lectures, and readings; the historic venue turns 85 in December 2013 / **GET YOUR ZYDECO ON** and come to the Grassroots Festival of Music and Dance in Trumansburg every summer (photo by Jeff Folkins) / Come to the **ITHACA FESTIVAL** music and arts celebration; pictured is the largest peace sign, made by 5,814 people (photo by Jon Reis) / **SHOP LOCAL AND ORGANIC** at GreenStar Cooperative Market (photo by Mariah Dahl) / **COME HUNGRY** to the sprawling Ithaca Farmer's Market, open on the lakefront every weekend from April to December (photo by Robert Barker) / Visit the **ITHACA CHILDREN'S GARDEN** that inspires, promotes, and sustains youth and community stewardship of the natural environment through garden-based learning and discovery; meet Gaia the giant turtle! (photo by Erin Marteal) / **COLLEGETOWN BAGELS** began in 1976 with a bagel and a dream; an Ithaca favorite featuring sandwiches, homemade entrées, salads, artisan breads and bagels, heavenly pastry, outstanding cheeses, and great coffee (photo by Alan Nyiri)

Ithaca is GORGES

The First-Year Experience at Cornell

Carol Grumbach '78, JD '87, associate dean, New Student Programs, Cornell University; the Jack and Rilla Neafsey Director, Carol Tatkon Center

Carol Grumbach '78, JD '87

"We have in place at Cornell a carefully designed First-Year Experience that is both a safety net and a gentle launching pad."

Invariably, when I ask an upper-level student to tell me about their first year at Cornell, they use two seemingly contradictory adjectives, such as "terrifying" and "exhilarating." They go on to say "but terrifying in a good way." When I ask them to elaborate, they explain that the first year was frightening not because bad things happened but because so much was unknown and new—and that is also exciting.

Such uncertainty can be difficult. There is good difficult and bad difficult, though, and it is crucial for new students and parents to sort out and discuss when students should figure out things on their own. We have in place at Cornell a carefully designed First-Year Experience that is both a safety net and a gentle launching pad. Incrementally and elaborately, we help new students make the transition to Cornell, navigate the university, and flourish. The offerings are amazing and unrecognizable to some people of previous generations.

The First-Year Experience starts with a five-day orientation designed to make the transition to Cornell as seamless as possible and introduce students to Cornell's academic, intellectual, cultural, co-curricular, and social opportunities. Students begin to acclimate to their new home and make new friends through small-group sessions with student

orientation leaders, floor meetings with student resident advisors, college sessions, and a host of social activities.

Through both university- and college-specific programs, new students are introduced to academic expectations and resources and services that support their academic goals and holistic well-being. Students are also introduced to the university's values—including Cornell's commitment to diversity and inclusion; the importance of integrity, academic honesty, and respect for intellectual ideas; and civic responsibility.

All first-year students live together on North Campus as part of a living-learning community that includes faculty-in-residence (who live with their families in the residences) and faculty fellows (who participate in intellectual and cultural programs). They play a pivotal role in helping students make meaningful connections with faculty, inspiring learning outside the classroom, making the residences a space for learning as well as living, and deepening students' intellectual experiences.

> "This spirit of intellectual exploration and passion for learning are the core of the First-Year Experience."

Central to North Campus is the Carol Tatkon Center, Cornell's intellectual, support, and resource center for first-year students. The center is run by upper-level students who act as mentors, and offers programs and services that help students transition to Cornell by promoting their well-being and academic success, sparking their intellectual curiosity, leading them to discover and explore new interests, and encouraging interaction with faculty outside of the classroom.

As you can see, we have so much support for new students, so I worry that some parents jump in a little too quickly to solve problems for their students. As a result, many students are less equipped than prior generations to direct and manage their lives. I encourage parents to pause and consider when they should step in. Definitely step in when your student is in distress, but perhaps not when they are solving problems, which is an extremely satisfying and essential skill. Do, however, prepare your student to live away from home. Ironically, it is sometimes the smallest of things—such as a lack of clean clothes—that causes the greatest stress. Make sure to teach your student how to handle the basics, like laundry.

Please do not do your student's work. This is a terrible idea for many reasons. First, your student needs to learn the material. If he or she doesn't, the opportunity to get an education has been wasted, and your student may suffer in later studies. Second, by helping, you may be causing your son or daughter to cheat. You do not want your student to be summoned to an academic integrity hearing board because you wanted to give his or her paper a quick edit. You also do not want your student to think that cheating is acceptable.

As a long-ago (and two-time) graduate of Cornell, I still remember my intellectual awakening in college. I hope that all parents encourage their new students to experience this intellectual coming of age and develop a passion for an area of study. Although it might not be easy to watch your student falter on occasion, be uncertain about his or her course of study, or even reject his or her original academic plan—hold tight, and let your student explore. This spirit of intellectual exploration and passion for learning are the core of the First-Year Experience, if not all years of study at Cornell.

FOR MORE INFORMATION
First-Year Experience: newstudentprograms.cornell.edu

2013 *Life on the Hill* student bloggers for cornell.edu/studentlife/blogs

Beyond the Classroom

Joseph A. Burke, PhD, associate dean of students, Cornell University; director, Residential Programs

Joseph Burke, PhD

"For most first-year students, the biggest adjustment to campus involves learning how to handle the newfound freedom that comes with living away from home."

While the benefits of a Cornell education are widely appreciated, parents and families often overlook how important out-of-classroom experiences are in preparing their students for life after graduation. Simply put, the educational experience at Cornell extends well beyond the classroom.

At Cornell, Residential Programs plays a large role in the living and learning that occurs in the residence halls. All first-year students live on North Campus in living-learning environments uniquely designed to attend to their needs. Our professional staff members (most with master degrees) live in the residence halls among the students, as do older students who are serving as resident advisors. Together, they help provide a safe, inclusive, and purposeful living and learning environment for new students.

The North Campus housing arrangement asserts an important university value. At its most basic level, it exposes students to the essence of community membership. Being a member of the Cornell community involves more than getting along with others, although it is an important skill to master, especially with those who are different than you. Membership in this community also carries with it the

responsibility to make contributions for the betterment of the whole. Residents are afforded the opportunity to take on leadership positions in their residence halls as well as on North Campus.

We often speak of "living and learning" or the "out-of-classroom experience." Regardless of the terminology, our underlying commitment remains the same: an obligation to the development of the whole student. The primacy of the academic mission is one that we take seriously, but we recognize that learning is not limited exclusively to that sphere. We understand that academic success is affected by what students do when they are not in class—participation

Left: Students walk through the Balch Hall archway on their way to summer classes

in student groups, sports, volunteer or paid work, and attendance to their overall health needs. Valuable learning takes place when our students are engaged in the life of their residence halls and the larger university community. Opportunities abound for involvement and contributions. Programmatic experiences allow residents to enhance their existing skills and also uncover and develop hidden talents. These opportunities help foster students' maturation as young adults— and they help foster a sense of community, as residents assume responsibility for enriching the well-being of others.

For most first-year students, the biggest adjustment to campus involves learning how to handle the newfound freedom that comes with living away from home. Many are challenged to make good decisions without the structure that living at home provided. Living on campus with the freedom to choose can initially overwhelm students with an almost endless series of decisions. Should I go out tonight? Get to bed early? Study? Take a walk? Watch TV? Go to the library? Hang out in the lounge? Attend a program in the hall? Initially, some will choose based on a whim or whatever seems most interesting in the moment.

To address the challenge, staff members in Residential Programs strive to help students learn to view their personal freedom and choices within the context of their own unique community. This perspective reflects our approach to living on campus: by placing individual decisions in the larger context of the educational community, students are encouraged to make choices in a more fruitful way. In other words, responsibility to the community helps anchor individual choice.

This concept is not new.

In 1940, on the occasion of the 75th anniversary of the charter of Cornell University, Carl Becker, the John Stambaugh Professor of History, illuminated the value of this approach in his address, titled "The Cornell Tradition: Freedom and Responsibility." Albeit, Becker was talking about the freedom and ensuing responsibility Cornell had given him as a member of the faculty, yet his central message

is as relevant and insightful today as it was then. Indeed, individual freedom comes with a responsibility to the community. The tension between individual freedom and community responsibility has existed since Aristotle's time—and probably even earlier, when the first humans gathered around a communal fire to ask: "How are we going to live together?"

Much of what we do in Residential Programs centers on trying to answer this question. Our staff members are committed to preparing students for their eventual roles as global citizens. We are steadfast in our goal of providing residence halls that are welcoming and supportive of all who come to Cornell. This is no small undertaking, as we attempt to create a living space that prudently balances the needs of the individual with those of the community.

Because Residential Programs is invested in providing a nurturing and challenging home environment for new students, we face some of the same challenges that parents do during their student's first-year experience. We try to strike the right balance between allowing your student to handle matters on his or her own (perhaps risking failure) and getting involved in his or her problem solving.

As a parent myself, one who has lived through sending two sons to college, I remember how my wife and I were often tempted to rescue our sons from uncertainty or try to solve their problems. The ease of technology has made that temptation even harder to resist. Like many parents, we battled "parental gravitational pull," that protective instinctual tug to get involved with all our children's struggles and shelter them from harm (regardless of the physical distance). We did so with the realization that we had to let each one find his way. Everything didn't always work out perfectly, but over the course of time, each of them became a more resilient and capable young adult. My colleagues in Residential Programs are aware of the necessity of striking such a balance with our new students, and we ask you to collaborate with us in using such an approach.

"Individual freedom comes with a responsibility to the community."

Encourage your first-year student to take some risks while he or she is at Cornell—not big risks at first, and not dangerous ones at all, but risks that require taking a step outside his or her comfort zone. Mistakes will be made, missteps will occur. But some of the errors our students make will deepen relationships, expand their understanding of community, and profoundly transform them as individuals. They will grow and benefit from their own mistakes—but not from the ones you make or protect them from.

In Residential Programs, we are dedicated to working with every student who lives on campus. We want your son or daughter to be successful and to reach full potential. The whole Cornell experience provides a solid foundation for individuals to realize success. Our promise is to continue to provide that strong foundation so that each student can find a fulfilling and valuable life.

FOR MORE INFORMATION
Living at Cornell: living.sas.cornell.edu

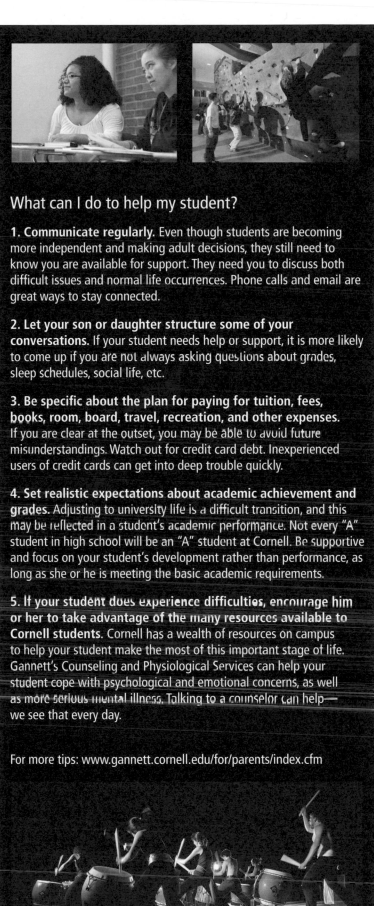

What can I do to help my student?

1. Communicate regularly. Even though students are becoming more independent and making adult decisions, they still need to know you are available for support. They need you to discuss both difficult issues and normal life occurrences. Phone calls and email are great ways to stay connected.

2. Let your son or daughter structure some of your conversations. If your student needs help or support, it is more likely to come up if you are not always asking questions about grades, sleep schedules, social life, etc.

3. Be specific about the plan for paying for tuition, fees, books, room, board, travel, recreation, and other expenses. If you are clear at the outset, you may be able to avoid future misunderstandings. Watch out for credit card debt. Inexperienced users of credit cards can get into deep trouble quickly.

4. Set realistic expectations about academic achievement and grades. Adjusting to university life is a difficult transition, and this may be reflected in a student's academic performance. Not every "A" student in high school will be an "A" student at Cornell. Be supportive and focus on your student's development rather than performance, as long as she or he is meeting the basic academic requirements.

5. If your student does experience difficulties, encourage him or her to take advantage of the many resources available to Cornell students. Cornell has a wealth of resources on campus to help your student make the most of this important stage of life. Gannett's Counseling and Physiological Services can help your student cope with psychological and emotional concerns, as well as more serious mental illness. Talking to a counselor can help—we see that every day.

For more tips: www.gannett.cornell.edu/for/parents/index.cfm

Living and Learning on West Campus

Scott MacDonald '78, PhD '86, the Dale R. Corson House Professor and Dean, Hans A. Bethe House; professor, Department of Philosophy, and the Norma K. Regan Professor in Christian Studies, College of Arts and Sciences

Scott MacDonald '78, PhD '86

"A Cornell education is rich in extraordinary opportunities; for students who live in one of the West Campus houses, the opportunities are mind opening and horizon broadening, and they are part of daily life."

On a Wednesday evening in October, Cornell professor Steve Strogatz is sitting on a couch in my living room telling a story. There are 25 students sitting around the room in armchairs and on the floor, most of them leaning slightly forward, elbows on knees, listening intently. Strogatz is a natural—relaxed, articulate, with a wry sense of humor—and the students are eating it up. If you were to walk into the room at this moment, you would sense instantly that something magical is happening.

The interesting part: Strogatz's story is illustrating a point about math (Strogatz works in applied mathematics and blogs about math for the *New York Times*), the living room is in my apartment in Hans Bethe House (one of five West Campus residential houses), and the students sitting around the room are residents of the house. Like every other Cornell undergraduate, these students can take Strogatz's courses and read his columns in the *Times*. But these students are hanging out with him, listening to his stories, and engaging with him in conversation while sitting in comfy chairs in the quiet informality of my living room. That kind of engagement with Strogatz can make your week, change the way you think about the world, maybe even change your life.

Conversations at Keeton with Steven Strogatz, professor of applied mathematics and director of the Center for Applied Mathematics

We do this sort of thing every Wednesday evening at Bethe House, and similar things happen regularly in each of the West Campus houses. On a Wednesday evening in November it's Mike Kaplitt, professor of neurological surgery at Weill Cornell Medical College, talking about the interface between brain science and surgery; on another Wednesday evening it's Paul Merrill, director of jazz ensembles, talking about jazz; on another it's Ritchie Patterson and Yuval Grossman, from the Department of Physics, talking about the discovery of the Higgs boson; on another it's Lyrae Van Clief-Stefanon, assistant professor of English, reading from her poetry.

Left: Hans A. Bethe House on West Campus

If comfy chairs are not your thing, or if you have a lab on Wednesday evenings, try this: dinner in the house dining room with Alfonso Torres, associate dean in the College of Veterinary Medicine; or David Feldshuh, professor of theatre; or Yervant Terzian, professor of astronomy. Or this: a bus trip to the Museum of Modern Art in New York City with a tour guided by Frank Robinson, legendary director emeritus of Cornell's Johnson Museum of Art. Or this: cooking with Mark Bittman, celebrated *New York Times* food columnist and best-selling author. Or this: a concert at Bailey Hall, or live jazz at the Carriage House.

When the pioneering founders of the West Campus house system envisioned residential houses that would be living-learning communities, they were imagining Cornell undergraduates engaging substantively, but informally, and on their own turf (in comfy chairs or at a dinner table in their own dining rooms), with Cornell faculty and distinguished campus visitors. To make that vision a reality they established five houses, a community of 1,800 students altogether, each house led by a live-in distinguished Cornell professor (the house professor and dean of the house) with the help of 30 associated Cornell faculty members (house fellows) charged with making magic happen in the house. That founding vision becomes reality in the living rooms of the house deans across West Campus, at dining tables in the house dining rooms, and in countless faculty-led activities and conversations that occur on a daily basis in the five West Campus houses. A Cornell education is rich in extraordinary opportunities; for students who live in one of the West Campus houses, the opportunities are mind opening and horizon broadening, and they are part of daily life.

Mark Bittman, celebrated *New York Times* food columnist and best-selling cookbook author, cooks with students at Bethe House

The West Campus house system is designed to be faculty led but also student run. On a Monday evening in the dining room, about 20 students are gathered over dinner for a weekly house council meeting. They are volunteers, active residents with interests, ideas, and energy for building community in the house. At this meeting they are doing detailed planning for upcoming events they are sponsoring: karaoke and bubble tea, the West Campus Café showcasing student performers, a trip to see the Yamatai Drumming concert, horseback riding lessons.

House Council is the formal student leadership group in the house, but student leadership takes many forms. The West Campus Active Citizens program acknowledges that fact. Active citizens earn that designation by demonstrating leadership in the house in a variety of

Partha Dasgupta, world-renowned economist, visited with students at Bethe House on a recent trip to campus as an A.D. White Professor-at-Large

Lyrae Van Clief-Stefanon, who teaches English and creative writing, reads from her poetry at a Literary Luncheon

ways—ways that make the house stronger, richer, and more diverse. They constitute the core of an engaged, vibrant community of residents.

Whatever else they are, the West Campus houses are also residences. They are safe and healthy places to eat, sleep, and study. The food is great—each house has its own dining room and chef. The buildings are comfortably appointed. And they are just a short (vertical) walk to central campus. But to think of West Campus as merely a place to live, even as a very nice place to live, is to overlook one of Cornell's great treasures. The faculty-led, student-run West Campus houses offer unparalleled opportunities for leadership and for intellectual, cultural, artistic, and social engagement. The West Campus living-learning experience can bring a Cornell education to life.

FOR MORE INFORMATION

West Campus House System:
   westcampushousesystem.cornell.edu
Dining at Cornell: living.sas.cornell.edu/dine
Living at Cornell: living.sas.cornell.edu/live

Co-ops: Hidden Jewels in Residential Living

Julie Paige, assistant dean of students, Office of Fraternities, Sororities, and Independent Living

Julie Paige

"Co-ops are some of the most caring living communities at Cornell."

It is your student's sophomore year, and you are driving the family to Cornell. Your student has chosen to live in one of the university-owned cooperatives and is very excited about this new living experience. You drive up and park in front of the house. It looks nice and well-kept on the outside. A co-op member opens the door and gives you both the warmest welcome. When you step inside, it's not what you expected. You think back to a year ago when you dropped your child off to their first-year residence hall, how perfect it looked—clean and fresh. Now, you're astonished by the mess you see and wonder how you can let your son or daughter live here.

If you have the opportunity to come back 10 days later, you'll feel like you are walking into a different house. The first weekend after classes begin is a co-op cleaning weekend, when house members form teams and deep clean their new home from top to bottom— this is their community-building experience. What you didn't know the

Von Cramm Hall

first time you opened the door is that co-ops are some of the most caring living communities. They are truly hidden jewels at Cornell.

I learned more about co-ops in 1991–1992 while I was serving as residence hall director for the newly formed Multicultural Living Unit. Watermargin, a co-op on West Campus, wanted to co-sponsor programs because our two living units shared similar values. I learned that Watermargin was created in 1947 by WWII veterans who came back to Cornell and found that Greek housing, at that time, was discriminatory toward African American and Jewish students. The veterans wanted housing that was open and welcoming.

In 2004, oversight of the co-ops became my responsibility, where I could provide additional programmatic leadership and training. Today, co-op leadership and the Division of Student and Academic Services—through the Office of Fraternities, Sororities, and Independent Living—work as partners.

An advantage of the university-owned co-ops —while they are run and governed by the students—is that they must conform to university safety standards. The houses are regularly inspected by the university, the City of Ithaca, and New York State. They are at full

Students relax on the Watermargin porch

The Wari Cooperative residence on North Campus

occupancy and regularly have students on waiting lists for a vacancy. They also have 24-hour/7-day-a-week access to Cornell University services such as Cornell University Police, Environmental and Health Safety, after hours facilities emergencies service, and the Residential Programs after-hours emergency on-call system. Students living in the co-ops sign Campus Life housing terms and conditions but are released midyear if they are participating in a Cornell-sponsored, off-campus study program, graduating early, or are required to leave the university.

I work with the co-op student leaders on a daily basis, beginning with a spring orientation program prior to the new academic year, extensive August and January training sessions, and monthly business meetings that include an in-service component. I work with co-op leaders on building community, getting to know all the students, and recognizing when a student may be in distress. I also serve as their contact for crisis management, and we work together to assure that co-op members are getting the resources they need to succeed at Cornell.

Working with the co-ops is one of the best parts of my life at Cornell.

Maintaining the Cooperative Spirit

In 2007, the Inter-Cooperative Council created a document titled "The Spirit of the Co-ops," describing the co-op system—it is excerpted here.

Working Definition of Co-ops at Cornell University

The eight university-owned and -managed buildings house within them independent and self-governed student organizations—Prospect of Whitby, 660 Stewart, 302 Wait Avenue Cooperative, Triphammer Cooperative, Von Cramm, Wait Terrace, Wari Cooperative, and Watermargin.

Although these organizations extend beyond the buildings in which they are based, their long histories and the personal investment of each resident in each building inexorably link the organizations to their physical structures. Through responsible action and leadership training leading to increased self-reliance, each co-op seeks to preserve its autonomy and maintain its facilities in partnership with the university.

Features

Co-ops offer a positive housing alternative to residence halls, program houses, off-campus housing, and fraternities/sororities. Each co-op is a unique, self-governed housing unit with distinctive features.

Benefits

The self-governing nature of co-ops demands respect, responsibility, and consideration from its residents. By taking personal responsibility for the upkeep of their organizations and facilities, co-op residents acquire practical, extracurricular training in building community that is not readily gained in traditional program houses or residence halls. This is how the cooperative spirit is built.

In addition, the open and supportive environment of co-ops fosters the development of student leadership skills through activism.

FOR MORE INFORMATION
Cooperative Housing at Cornell: living.sas.cornell.edu/live/
wheretolive/co-ops, co-ops@cornell.edu

"Living off campus has been quite the experience. There are definitely both pros and cons. The pros have been the privacy. I don't have to deal with parents and siblings, or roommates. I have a place that's all mine. The cons have been the bills and the cleaning! You have to stay on top of everything. Living off campus is a mixture of the college life and real life. For me, it's the perfect balance between remaining a kid and becoming an adult."
—Savannah Sims '14,
College of Arts and Sciences

Living Off Campus: Rewards and New Experiences

Denise Thompson, off-campus housing coordinator, Office of Fraternities, Sororities, and Independent Living

Denise Thompson

"I meet with students on a daily basis to guide them through the off-campus housing search process. During the initial meeting, I try to empower students to own and enjoy this new journey."

Students who move off campus are often most successful when they are informed and understand the expectations of their new community, landlord, neighbors, roommates. It is important that our students remember they are members of a community and should work together to get the most from this experience.

Our goal in providing off-campus housing services is to maintain a programmatic and support focus, assisting students by offering appropriate resources.

I meet with students on a daily basis to guide them through the off-campus housing search process. During the initial meeting, I try to empower students to own and enjoy this new journey. We review the *New York State Tenants' Rights Guide*, consider the different neighborhoods in the area, and discuss what it means to be a successful tenant and neighbor. We talk about the importance of choosing a compatible roommate and understanding financial responsibilities. As they begin to understand the implications associated with signing a legal contract, the students I work with want to be successful tenants. I enjoy working with all students who come to my office, advising them about how to begin the housing search process, communicate with an unresponsive landlord, or resolve a roommate conflict.

Savannah Sims '14

There is plenty of rental housing available in the Ithaca area. One can live on a busy city street or in a quiet family neighborhood. Students should explore all their housing options before rushing to sign a lease. During a student's first year at Cornell, their social and academic network will expand and change multiple times. By waiting to sign a lease, students will have the opportunity to learn more about Cornell, the Ithaca area, and each other, thus allowing them to make more informed and desirable housing decisions.

We provide our students with the tools, services, resources, and referrals to create a safe and healthy home.

FOR MORE INFORMATION
Off-Campus Living: offcampushousing.cornell.edu,
    ocho@cornell.edu

CRUCIAL RESOURCES

Many of us who work in college health have experienced first-hand the myriad of emotions that you may feel during your student's time at Cornell. Excitement, worry, trepidation, pride: they come at every stage of the college experience.

—Janet Corson-Rikert, MD

Above: Parents listen to President David J. Skorton at the 2012 New Student Convocation

Left: Diversity Hosting Weekend registration

Living Well To Learn Well

Janet Corson-Rikert, MD, executive director, Gannett Health Services; associate vice president, Campus Health, Cornell University

Janet Corson-Rikert, MD

"We encourage you to open the door to conversations about some of the tougher health topics—including stress, sexuality, relationships, alcohol and other drugs, emotional well-being, and dealing with concern for others."

Many of us who work in college health have experienced first-hand the myriad of emotions that you may feel during your student's time at Cornell. Excitement, worry, trepidation, pride: they come at every stage of the college experience. Such feelings may be most intense at times when students are challenged by experiences that directly affect their physical or emotional well-being. At these times, you may feel acutely aware of the direct correlation between your student's overall health and his or her academic success. As Herophilus, personal physician to Alexander the Great, once said, "When health is absent, wisdom cannot reveal itself, art cannot become manifest, strength cannot fight, wealth becomes useless, and intelligence cannot be applied."

Cornell's talented and diverse student body and world-class faculty will introduce your son or daughter to a marvelous array of perspectives and opportunities. During the first year of college, parents will glimpse the beginnings of great personal, social, and intellectual unfolding in their children. And throughout the college journey, parents will get progressive practice in the challenging process of letting go.

Gannett Health Services staff members

Letting go is not easy. It's not easy to entrust our son's or daughter's care to others. It's not easy to be confident they will know when, where, and how to reach out for help. Let me assure you that my colleagues and I at Gannett Health Services are invested in your student's health and well-being. We have chosen to specialize in college student health because we genuinely enjoy college students and believe that good health maximizes their quality of life and academic success.

Gannett is located on central campus, and we provide user-friendly primary care services for students when they are in Ithaca.

Left: Student life at Cornell

As a pediatrician specializing in adolescent medicine, I have found this community a rewarding place to practice medicine. We are very fortunate at Gannett to have an interdisciplinary staff that specializes in providing high-quality, integrated medical, mental health, and health promotion services that are specifically geared to the needs of emerging young adults who live in an intense learning environment. Together we are able to treat the whole person, recognizing the interconnections of emotional and physical health as well as addressing health concerns in the context of students' academic and social lives.

Gannett is fully accredited by the Accreditation Association for Ambulatory Health Care and has been recognized by the National Committee for Quality Assurance for having achieved the highest level of certification as a patient-centered medical home. This designation reflects the commitment of our healthcare team to maximize quality of care, access to services, communication, and care coordination. We are proud of the fact that Gannett is one of the first university health services nationally to achieve this status.

Many first-year students come to us as soon as they arrive on campus to arrange for ongoing medical and psychological care, allergy shots, and immunizations. Other students take advantage of our specialty clinics, including sports medicine, travel medicine, an eating disorder program, and sexuality services. Gannett is open to students Monday–Saturday during regular business hours, and we are also available for phone consultation 24 hours a day, seven days a week, at 607-255-5155. Our website provides a robust overview of our services as well as our approach to care.

For emergency or life-threatening situations of any kind, students should call the Cornell Police at 607-255-1111 (or 911) and request an ambulance. A response team will assess the situation and, if needed, transport the student to our local Ithaca hospital, Cayuga Medical Center. If a student experiences an illness or injury (or observes someone else in trouble) and needs advice, he or she can consult by phone with the police or with a Gannett healthcare provider (any time of day or night), and the provider will recommend next steps. This may involve transport to the hospital, but it may also involve

Some staff members from the Gannett Flu Crew who helped deliver nearly 10,000 immunizations during flu season

a next-day appointment at Gannett or with another local healthcare provider. Gannett's website has an extensive section devoted to the management of urgent health situations.

As a parent, you recognize that your daughter or son should have health insurance coverage that assures maximum access to care with minimal barriers. Without such coverage, unexpected medical expenses could alter your student's future.

Selecting an effective health insurance plan is one of the most important ways you can support your student's well-being. We encourage students and their families to become informed consumers of healthcare with knowledge and understanding of how their health insurance works. Cornell's annual enrollment/waiver process is an opportune time to discuss health insurance, healthcare costs, and health-related issues—and make sure your daughter or son has the coverage she or he will need. What will it cover and how will it work at Cornell, in Ithaca, and at other destinations your student travels to for study, work, or recreation? Will it facilitate timely and confidential access to affordable healthcare? How does it compare to Cornell's Student Health Insurance Plan?

In the United States, family health insurance plans are required to offer coverage for children up to the age of 26. However, many do not provide adequate coverage for students who are living away from home and who are "out of area." Others have high deductibles or out-of-pocket costs that make students hesitant to seek needed care.

More than half of our students are enrolled in Cornell's Student Health Insurance Plan (SHIP). Cornell's SHIP is broadly recognized as a model student health insurance program. The plan is carefully crafted by a committee of students, faculty, and staff to address student healthcare needs, meet Cornell's requirements, assure access to Ithaca-area medical specialists, and meet the varied needs of those traveling to other parts of the country and the world.

In the present healthcare environment, Gannett is not able to participate with or directly bill most health insurance plans. With more than 1,700 different plans covering our diverse student body, the costs of the infrastructure required to support insurance billing would require a disproportionate share of the resources available for student healthcare. We invest these critical resources in our medical and counseling services. All full-time registered students, regardless of their health insurance plan, can meet with a Gannett healthcare provider or counselor for a nominal $10 student user fee. Charges for most other services at Gannett are covered for those enrolled in the SHIP (see the Office of Student Health Insurance website for more details). For students who have private health insurance, bills for lab tests, X-rays, procedures, and medications are provided online and may be submitted to private insurance for potential reimbursement. We also offer use of the student bursar system to minimize any financial barriers to accessing services.

The 2012 Sexual Harassment Prevention Resource Fair

Parents have a very important role in helping students make decisions about protecting their health and seeking healthcare. In a recent survey, students confirmed what we guessed: they want to be able to turn to their parents first to talk about health-related concerns. We also observe them in sensitive situations in which they don't want to worry their parent or risk disapproval, or where they just want to handle something on their own. We encourage you to open the door to conversations about some of the tougher health topics, including stress, sexuality, relationships, alcohol and other drugs, emotional well-being, and dealing with concern for others. The Gannett website has a wealth of information on these topics, written especially for parents, and we hope you will review it when the time seems right.

If your student has an ongoing physical or mental health concern, I recommend that you and your student discuss connecting with a healthcare provider at Gannett before an urgent need arises. Gannett is well prepared to support students with many chronic conditions, such as allergies and asthma, diabetes, eating disorders, and depression and other mental health concerns.

Even students who arrive on campus without a history of significant illness or injury can benefit from a parental nudge to prioritize their health. We know from experience that students often put off seeking care for a "small" problem and then end up missing classes, work, and other important activities as the problem escalates. Please join us in helping your student learn how to make effective and timely use of the many health resources available. We have found that it is helpful for students and parents to discuss healthcare access ahead of actual need; for instance, how and when to use health services, communicate with a healthcare provider or counselor, submit bills to insurance for reimbursement, and more.

The majority of undergraduates entering Cornell are around 18 years of age. This means that they are now able to vote, serve in the armed forces, and make legally binding adult decisions. Among these is the right to make medical decisions and sign their own medical consents. This can be a challenging adjustment for parents and students alike, given that parents are typically the primary organizing and deciding forces who guide students' healthcare from birth until college.

We encourage students to involve their families in health matters. In emergency situations, we may exercise authority to contact you ourselves. Otherwise, federal and state privacy laws require us to have your student's written consent to talk with you about issues related to his or her healthcare (including bills).

Establishing a sense of privacy is vital to the trust between healthcare providers and the patients/clients they serve. Recent survey results show 50 percent of Cornell students have concerns about privacy and nearly 20 percent of Cornell students have actually avoided seeking healthcare as a result of those concerns. The percentage is higher among students enrolled in their parents' health insurance plans. Students on Cornell's Student Health Insurance Plan are the actual policy owners and receive their own bills from healthcare providers, but for students enrolled in family health plans, bills are typically sent to parents. Students tend to feel most anxious about privacy and confidentiality when seeking care related to sensitive health topics (e.g., sexual health, substance use, mental health concerns, etc.). Please remind your student that you respect his or her privacy and that you want your son or daughter to feel no hesitation in asking for help when it is needed.

Although law and standards of care prevent us from discussing your student's healthcare without a signed release, confidentiality laws do not limit what you can say to us. Please do not hesitate to share your observations and concerns. We may be able to help you troubleshoot the situation by phone. You may also call with general questions about our services and/or our approach to care. Over time, we hope you and your family will come to view confidentiality as an asset, one that helps students talk openly with our healthcare providers and develop a sense of confidence in making decisions that benefit their self-care and well-being.

On behalf of my colleagues at Gannett, welcome to the Cornell community. We look forward to working with you as partners in supporting the health and well-being of your student.

FOR MORE INFORMATION
Health Emergencies: www.gannett.cornell.edu/emergencies
Gannett Health Services: www.gannett.cornell.edu
Gannett Health Services 24/7 phone counseling: 607-255-5155
Health information for parents/guardians:
    www.gannett.cornell.edu/for/parents
"Tough Topics" on mental health, alcohol, sex, and more:
    www.gannett.cornell.edu/for/parents/tough
"Insurance Matters" parent information about student health insurance:
    www.gannett.cornell.edu/for/parents/insurance.cfm
Office of Student Health Insurance: studentinsurance.cornell.edu

Navigating the Transition to University Life

Greg Eells, PhD, director, Counseling and Psychological Services; associate director, Gannett Health Services

Greg Eells, PhD

"Counseling and Psychological Services is a resource that can help students navigate this evolving landscape and the stress it sometimes produces."

In becoming a member of the Cornell community, your son or daughter has taken a significant step toward life as a more autonomous adult. He or she may now experience daily the fact that "the world gets bigger as we go along." This normal and important part of students' growth and development may be very exciting. It may also feel a bit scary at times, especially if your student experiences mental health difficulties along the way. A growing consensus suggests that more students do experience such difficulties. Some arrive on college and university campuses with existing mental health difficulties. Research also indicates that some mental illnesses begin to manifest themselves for the first time in the traditional college-age population. Thankfully, research also indicates that the sooner a young person receives supportive services and/or treatment, the better his or her long-term prognosis will be.

Cornell University takes a comprehensive public health approach to addressing student mental health, including a range of environmental strategies, education, and direct services. Our campus services are designed to assist students in navigating this time in their personal development and in making this significant transition to adulthood.

These services and resources include academic advising and support, residential programs, the Office of the Dean of Students, and more. Counseling and Psychological Services (CAPS), a department of Gannett Health Services, provides consultation, support, and services related to mental health. While most students receive one-on-one or group counseling services and/or medication management at Gannett Health Services, they also can consult with CAPS counselors during the "Let's Talk" hours at several different locations around campus.

What works for students?

Though many Cornell services provided to students require the student simply to show up to meet their needs (e.g., dining, transportation and parking services, etc.), mental health services are more like their academic work or their fitness center membership. To get the most out of mental healthcare, the student must be an ongoing and active participant in the process. Parents and family members serve as essential supports to a student working to manage mental health difficulties. They can assist the student by expressing concern and directing them to appropriate resources. They can also express hope about how seeking help and working with providers can make the situation better.

> "Though the transition to university life can be challenging, it also is a very exciting time."

There are a variety of different approaches to counseling, and students' experiences can vary considerably depending on the counselor they see. In general, most approaches to counseling are designed to help people "accept what is" and "pursue what matters." To assist students in accepting what is, counselors work to create a structured, supportive, and safe environment to help their clients respond more flexibly to their thoughts and feelings. They also work to model and cultivate patience and self-compassion. The pursuing what matters component of counseling often involves working with clients to set small, realistic goals for what they want to accomplish and to set aside time between sessions to reflect on issues discussed during visits, complete readings, or take part in other supportive activities. If at any point a student has a concern about the counseling process, it is best the student address the concern with his or her counselor or group as soon as possible.

Given what parents and professionals know of students' varying levels of maturity and self-reliance, it can be surprising to learn that, legally, college students are adults with federal and state privacy protections for information about their healthcare. In other words, if a student is agreeable to letting parents or family members know about his or her mental healthcare, he or she can sign a release of information allowing their mental health providers to talk to designated family members. However, if a student does not want his or her parent or family member to know about such care, it is his or her legal right to keep such information private. It also means that parents or family members cannot make appointments for students, nor confirm if the students attended their scheduled counseling or psychiatry visits. This can be frustrating for parents or guardians who have concerns about the well-being of their students. However, please know that if a CAPS mental health professional feels that involving a family member can help secure a student whom they feel may be at imminent risk, the provider will make a professional decision to involve the family.

Though the transition to university life can be challenging, it also is a very exciting time. Students have the opportunity to interact with others from diverse backgrounds. They also have the opportunity to be challenged both intellectually and personally in ways they may not have been challenged before. CAPS is a resource that can help students navigate this evolving landscape and the stress it sometimes produces. It also provides students with tools and insight to manage the tough times and make the most of the opportunities life presents.

FOR MORE INFORMATION

Counseling and Psychological Services:
   www.gannett.cornell.edu/CAPS
Cornell's Mental Health Framework:
   www.gannett.cornell.edu/campus/welfare/framework.cfm
Stress by Year: www.gannett.cornell.edu/topics/stress/manage/year
How to support your student in distress:
   www.gannett.cornell.edu/notice/roles/parents.cfm
Resources for students in distress:
   www.gannett.cornell.edu/notice/resources
Gannett Health Services 24/7 phone counseling: 607-255-5155
Gannett Health Services information for parents/guardians:
   www.gannett.cornell.edu/for/parents

From: www.gannett.cornell.edu/topics/stress/manage/year

General themes in college stress
- First-year floundering
- Sophomore slump
- Juggling it all as a junior
- Senioritis and saying goodbye
- Transfer tricks
- Graduate grief

Self-Esteem Is Key

Tanni Hall '76, MEd, associate dean of students, Cornell University; director, Office of Student and Community Support

Tanni Hall '76

"Encourage your student to express himself or herself. And be a really good listener when his or her views are different from yours! Allow your student to make choices, take responsibility for those choices, and learn from individual decisions."

Congratulations, and welcome to the Cornell family.

I am fortunate to have the opportunity to work closely with students, staff, and faculty to deliver a diverse array of programs and services that extend across campus in support of student well-being. Our goals are to promote personal growth, respectful human relations, and appreciation of diversity—and to enhance each student's ability to thrive and contribute to a vibrant, inclusive educational community.

My office provides professional- and peer-led programs that focus on student interaction and offer personal support and advocacy, training and education, outreach and community building, and volunteer and leadership development.

A key component for your student's academic and personal success and enjoyment at Cornell is self-esteem. And I am passionate about this topic. (I first learned of a model for increasing self-esteem from author and educator Sidney Simon—and I have been building upon it ever since.)

Self-esteem is a consistent self-image and internal sense of self-confidence and self-acceptance—it is influenced, but not determined, by the outside world.

Common sense tells us that high self-esteem is a good thing—and of course there is much research that supports our common sense. People with high self-esteem are more resilient to life's difficulties and setbacks and less likely to give in to despair or defeat; they take better care of their physical and mental health; they are more motivated and successful in life, believe they can achieve their goals, are better able to see the good in others and the world around them; and they are happier, more optimistic, and able to give of themselves to others.

Left: A student practices slacklining outside Myron Taylor Hall

This model describes seven conditions for self-esteem. You may notice that they all overlap and interconnect, and a change in one will affect all the others. Opportunities abound at Cornell to increase self-esteem with each of these conditions. We hope that you will encourage your son or daughter to pursue these opportunities:

1. Role models and mentors. These are people who inspire you, who see your potential, bring out the best in you, and help you along the way.

At Cornell, your student will have many opportunities for finding role models and mentors—they may be faculty members, residence hall staff, advisors for activities, other students involved in their classes or activities, or people in the campus community with whom they interact regularly. And your student will have opportunities to become a role model or mentor for others, as well.

2. Sense of accomplishment, contribution, and productivity. Ever notice how you can work, work, work, or study, study, study and still feel like you haven't accomplished anything at the end of the day? The key to overcoming this feeling is to do something different from what you typically do each day.

Encourage your student to avoid extremes, such as over-studying and overloading on activities, to avoid perfectionism, and to seek balance in order to feel an internal sense of accomplishment. Giving of themselves to help others is another great way they can feel a sense of accomplishment and feel that they're making a difference.

3. Risk. Taking small risks (not big or dangerous ones), guided by common sense and skill level, brings you outside your comfort zone and enhances personal growth. There are all sorts of possibilities to consider: social, emotional, physical, intellectual, spiritual.

Encourage your student to explore outside his or her comfort zone. What is the small risk out there waiting for him or her to take? Speaking up in class? Asking someone to lunch? Taking a class in an unfamiliar subject? Getting to know someone who seems different from the people he or she usually hangs out with?

4. Feeling special or unique. We all need to feel like someone who really matters.

You can show your son or daughter this condition in every conversation you have. Find at least one positive and unique thing about your student, the more specific the better, and tell him or her each time you talk together—a quality or trait you respect or admire, a special talent you notice, something you enjoy about him or her, etc. It will make you feel great, too.

5. Sense of belonging and connectedness. Meaningful friendships and connections with others, both individuals and groups, enhance our self-esteem.

As students transition away from home and into their new world at Cornell, parents can support them in seeking out a sense of belonging and feeling "at home"—in classes, residence halls, clubs, activities, jobs, volunteer opportunities, sports, etc. Encourage balance: remind your student not to rely on just one person, yet also not to get stretched thin with too many other obligations, including social ones.

6. Sense of empowerment. Making choices and decisions— and accepting responsibility for them, regardless of how they turn out—is one of the most powerful ways to increase self-esteem.

Self-expression is another—feeling empowered to express our unique thoughts, ideas, talents, and feelings without allowing fears, such as fear of judgment from others or fear of failure, to hold us back. Encourage your student to express himself or herself. And be a really good listener when his or her views are different from yours! Allow your student to make choices, take responsibility for those choices, and learn from individual decisions.

7. Enjoyment, humor, and passion. Life shouldn't be all work and no play. Enjoyment and levity can make our lives richer and more fulfilling.

Encourage your student to take time for fun and laugher—and for doing some things simply for pure enjoyment and to follow his or her life passions.

The 2011 *Tapestry of Possibilities* theatrical presentation and moderated discussion

The following programs are sponsored by the Office of Student and Community Support, Staley Center, Willard Straight Hall:

Cornell Minds Matter—A student-run mental health advocacy program dedicated to helping Cornell students deal with stress, lead a balanced existence, and use challenges and opportunities for growth and success: mindsmatter.dos.cornell.edu

Cornell Women's Resource Center—Offers resources and referral, support, educational programming, advocacy, and outreach aimed at ending sexism and all forms of oppression: wrc.dos.cornell.edu, womensresctr-mailbox@cornell.edu

Empathy, Assistance, and Referral Service (EARS)—Training, outreach workshops, and phone and drop-in counseling: ears@cornell.edu; or reach the peer counseling line at 607-255-3277

Muslim Cultural Center—A space for students to explore the Muslim culture and their cultural identity, regardless of their religion, and to promote the diversity and richness of the Muslim community on campus

Ordinary People Peer Education Theater Ensemble—Delivers performances of high-impact and often hilarious material to initiate discussions about human interactions

Tapestry of Possibilities: Diversity at Cornell—a mandatory orientation program and presentation for first-year and transfer students; performed by the Ordinary People theater ensemble: tapestry.dos.cornell.edu

Members of the women's polo team at Oxley Equestrian Center

Drug Use and Addictive Behavior

Ron Harris-Warrick, professor, Department of Neurobiology and Behavior, College of Arts and Sciences;
Stephen H. Weiss Presidential Fellow

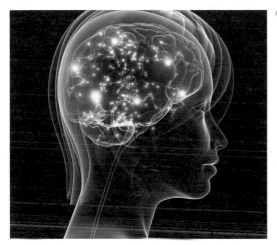

"One of the slowest brain regions to mature is the frontal cortex, which is responsible for high-level cognition and decision-making. As a consequence, college students have more trouble controlling impulses and making decisions."

The college years are a time of maximal exploration and risk-taking when many students try out hang gliding, rock climbing, and extreme skiing. This is also a time when many students experiment with psychoactive drugs, including alcohol, marijuana, and other illicit drugs. As with other risky behaviors, drug use peaks in the late teens and early 20s and declines rapidly after that time. This reflects, in part, the incomplete development of the adolescent brain, which continues to refine its connections and its network wiring into the early to mid 20s.

One of the slowest brain regions to mature is the frontal cortex, which is responsible for high-level cognition and decision-making. As a consequence, college students have more trouble controlling impulses and making decisions. As psychologist Laurence Steinberg wrote, a teenager's brain "has a well-developed accelerator but only a partly developed brake." The resulting impulsive behavior leads to thoughtless decisions and a slightly greater preference than adults for smaller, near-term goals over larger, long-term goals. All of these factors lead to increased drug use during the college years.

While this is a cause for family concern, parents should not assume the worst. Drug use among college students is not as high as you might imagine.

Cornell University carried out a survey of drug use by its students in 2010, which showed that they typically use drugs at levels slightly below the national averages. For example, in a typical month, while 70 percent of Cornell students had at least one drink, only eight percent were smokers, 11 percent smoked marijuana, and one percent used amphetamines; all other drugs were used by less than one percent of our students. Thus, the odds are that your son or daughter will drink alcohol at least occasionally. However, only a small percentage of our students use any other drugs. You can emphasize this to your student: drug use is the exception rather than the rule. If someone comes up to him or her at a party and offers a drug and says "everyone is using it," this person is not telling the truth.

The most common and the most dangerous drugs used at colleges are alcohol and tobacco. Nicotine in tobacco is one of the most addictive drugs known to man. Of adolescents who have smoked at least four cigarettes, 94 percent go on to become regular smokers who are addicted to nicotine. While the psychoactive effects of nicotine are mild, its addictive properties keep people smoking and thus expose

Left: Ron Harris-Warrick with specimens from the Wilder Brain Collection

them to harmful carcinogens and compounds that greatly elevate the risk for cancer, emphysema, and other diseases. Every year, more than 440,000 people die in the United States from the effects of smoking. The average adult smoker dies 14 years earlier than a non-smoker, and the American Cancer Society estimates that one half of all people who smoke their entire life will die from a smoking-related illness such as cancer. It is very difficult to stop smoking, despite Mark Twain's statement: "It's easy to quit smoking. I've done it hundreds of times." Only three to five percent of smokers succeed in quitting in any year. The best solution is never to start.

Alcohol is the major drug of abuse at Cornell—and the focus of the President's Council on Alcohol and Other Drugs, which meets monthly to design programs to reduce drug use at Cornell. Alcohol is one of the most lethal drugs used in America. Every year, about 35,000 people die as a direct result of alcohol use, while another 41,000 die as an indirect consequence of alcohol-induced violence or accidents. Alcohol is a major factor in 70 percent of homicides and 10 percent of auto fatalities. Alcohol dramatically reduces basic judgment and impulse control. Many of our tragic accidental deaths at Cornell are related to alcohol overuse, and alcohol is a major factor in unsafe sexual behavior, fights, and other violence. Addiction is a major problem, too. About one in six drinkers become alcoholics, whose lives circle around obtaining alcohol to the detriment of their careers, families, and lifestyle.

"The most common and most dangerous drugs used at colleges are alcohol and tobacco."

Compared to alcohol and tobacco, illicit drugs pose minor risks to college students. Marijuana is by far the major illicit drug of abuse, but less than one in five students smokes with any regularity. Smoking marijuana does not have lethal consequences like abusing alcohol does. While there is a lethal dose for half of drinkers in a bottle of whiskey, a person would have to smoke almost 150 pounds of marijuana at once to die. Epidemiologically, unlike tobacco, marijuana smoking is not linked to any diseases, perhaps because marijuana users smoke far fewer cigarettes per day than tobacco smokers do. However, marijuana does reduce judgment and distorts visual and temporal perception, making it dangerous to smoke and drive.

Another illicit group of drugs, amphetamines, are sometimes used as study aids, though only by a small percentage of non-ADHD (attention-deficit hyperactivity disorder) students at Cornell. These drugs are typically taken at very low doses, which are not dangerous. Other illicit drugs (cocaine, heroin, and psychedelics such as LSD and ecstasy) are only used by a very tiny fraction of Cornell students.

Why are all these drugs so pleasurable and addictive? It is not simply that they make you feel good; all of them also have direct actions in the brain that makes the brain want more. All the addictive drugs—including nicotine, alcohol, cocaine, and heroin—act to enhance the activity of the so-called "dopamine reward pathway." Dopamine is a neurotransmitter in the brain, released from one neuron onto other neurons to change their activity and communicate in the networks that drive brain function. The reward pathway arises from a set of dopaminergic neurons in the midbrain, which send processes forward to the nucleus accumbens, frontal cortex, and elsewhere. Rewarding stimuli, such as food, drink, and sex, naturally excite these dopaminergic neurons. Recent research has shown that they signal the relative value of a reward, compared to the expected value of that reward. For example, if a hungry animal suddenly gets food, the reward is greater than expected and the dopamine neurons fire. However, if the reward is fully expected (for example, when an animal learns to perform a task for the food reward), these neurons do not fire, and if the reward is less than expected (for example, when the animal performs the learned task but is not given the food), these neurons reduce their firing rate. Activity in these neurons thus serves as a learning signal to practice behaviors that lead to better rewards.

All the addictive drugs hijack this dopamine pathway by activating it directly, rather than through the normal neural pathways between sensory perception and appreciation. Therefore, taking drugs produces a brain signal that tells us the reward is always better than expected and provides a very powerful learning signal: keep taking the drug. From this perspective, drug addiction can be understood as an aberrant form of learning. Eventually, other pathways are activated as one progresses to full addiction, leading to many long-term changes in brain function. These changes can reverse back to normal when a person quits using the drug, but only very slowly over a period of years of abstinence. This is why it is so difficult to quit smoking, drinking, or using drugs.

However, addiction is not inevitable, and there appear to be strong individual differences in susceptibility to drug addiction. For example, only one in four people who ever try heroin go on to be addicts, and only one in six people who try cocaine or alcohol become addicts. All of us know people who are capable of regular, moderate drinking and do not progress to socially inappropriate drunkenness or addiction, while others who start the same way cannot control their drinking. Scientists are not sure what underlies this different susceptibility, but growing evidence indicates that genetic predisposition can play a major role. Some people are born with a genetic makeup that makes it easier for them to progress to inappropriate drug use and addiction while others do not.

If drinking has caused problems in your family (one in four families in the United States has a problem drinker), it is very important that your son or daughter be cautious about alcohol use. Weaker evidence suggests that some genetic factors may affect susceptibility to addiction in general; most addicts, for example, are addicted to more than one drug. If addiction to any drug is a family problem, your sons and daughters should be cautious about using drugs.

"Cornell students typically use drugs at levels slightly below national averages."

Addiction is not limited to drug abuse. Some people show addictive-type behaviors for other stimuli, including pornography, gambling, video games, and even cellphone use. This can become a problem when these behaviors start to interfere with normal activities, causing users to focus their actions around their addiction to the exclusion of other normally rewarding activities. These addictive behaviors can also activate the dopamine reward pathway, and while it is not yet clear whether this is a first step in leading to behavioral addiction, many scientists predict that this will be found to be true.

What can your family do if your son or daughter starts experimenting with drugs? First of all, it is important not to panic. As described above, drug use is a temporary behavior for the large majority of all adolescents who experiment, and most of them grow out of it as their brains mature and the demands of adult life arise. Try to maintain open lines of communication to check that your son or daughter is remaining positive about his or her studies, has good social interactions with other students, and maintains strong interest in extracurricular activities. Marked reduction in interest in all activities can be a danger sign of many things, including depression, but could also result from unregulated drug use.

"Our efforts are aimed at helping students return to normal and productive activities and are not punitive in nature."

Cornell has many resources to help identify and support students in distress, including students who have had incidents of alcohol or drug overuse. Our efforts are aimed at helping students return to normal and productive activities and are not punitive in nature. If families encounter a major problem, the university encourages them to interact with Cornell's resources and programs to help support their student.

National Trends in Drug Use

The group Monitoring the Future (monitoringthefuture.org) has followed national trends in drug use since the 1970s by using very large-scale annual surveys of student drug use.

- Alcohol use has been falling slowly. In 2011, about two-thirds of college students had at least one drink each month, but only 40 percent had been drunk at least once during the previous month.

- Smoking has also fallen. Only 15 percent of college students smoke regularly.

- In general, illicit drug use has remained steady or declined slightly over the past 15 years, with no obvious epidemic of rising drug use in the recent past.

- Nationally, about one in five college students used any illicit drug more than once a month; most of these drugs were marijuana (17 percent of students), amphetamines (five percent), or opioid prescription drugs such as oxycodone (six percent).

- Only one percent or fewer of college students used any other drugs such as cocaine, heroin, hallucinogens, or ecstasy with any frequency.

Alcohol and Social Life at Cornell

Tim Marchell, director, Mental Health Initiatives; associate director, Gannett Health Services

Tim Marchell

"The more the university and parents can do together to educate students about the risks related to alcohol, the more prepared students will be to navigate any challenges they face."

Alcohol is part of the social scene at Cornell as it is at colleges and universities across the country. Many students enjoy drinking, and some engage in it as part of their transition to adulthood, even though it is illegal for them to do so if they are under the age of 21. Certainly our society exposes them to many messages that convey that drinking is "fun and cool."

Because students' health and safety is of utmost important to us, Cornell undertakes efforts to prevent alcohol-related problems and encourages parents to talk with their sons and daughters about the role of alcohol in their college experiences. The more the university and parents can do together to educate students about the risks related to alcohol, the more prepared students will be to navigate any challenges they face.

The good news is that research shows most Cornell students tend to drink in moderation or not at all (e.g., more than half either do not drink or typically have three or fewer drinks in a sitting). Our students also hold some important, positive attitudes about the use of alcohol. For example, most students believe it is never socially acceptable to drink to the point of "blacking out."

There is another reality, however, which is that alcohol (along with other drugs) contributes to far too many negative consequences for a significant number of our students and those around them. In a given year, three in 10 will drink to the point of having memory loss. Alcohol also commonly plays a role in physical fights, unprotected sex, sexual assaults, and vandalism. Students who drink heavily often regret their behavior, which includes missing classes and doing poorly on their academic work as a result of a long night out. And nearly every weekend, some students drink to the point of alcohol poisoning that requires emergency medical treatment. As we know from experience, the consequences of heavy drinking can be fatal.

Preventing high-risk drinking and the harm it causes requires a comprehensive approach that includes educating students, re-shaping the environment in which they make decisions about drinking, and providing services to those who develop drinking problems. The university's primary efforts, guided by our President's Council on Alcohol and Other Drugs, include the following:

- All incoming first-year students are expected to complete an online educational program about alcohol before arriving on campus.

- We restrict access to alcohol through policies; for example, placing a ban on first-year students from attending fraternity events with alcohol during the fall semester.

- We host late-night (after 11 p.m.) events on campus that offer alternatives to unregulated parties with alcohol.

Left: Cornell's annual Slope Day event, held in May, during which students 21 and older are permitted to drink alcohol

- In addition to enforcing the minimum drinking age of 21, our residence hall rules forbid underage students from being in the presence of alcohol even if they are not drinking.

- At Gannett Health Services, we screen for alcohol problems during primary care medical visits and refer students to our alcohol specialists in Counseling and Psychological Services.

- When students call for help in alcohol- or drug-related emergencies, our Good Samaritan Protocol and New York State law exempt them and the ill person from charges related to underage drinking and low-level drug possession.

- Students who violate our alcohol policies must complete BASICS, the scientifically validated Brief Alcohol Screening and Intervention for College Students program.

We continue to explore new ways to deal with the ongoing challenges posed by alcohol. One of the most important and promising approaches is to enlist the support of parents. We know some parents believe that by the time their son or daughter is ready to head off to college, their opportunity to influence his or her decisions in relation to alcohol has passed. Yet parents can—and do—continue to shape their student's choices on this and other critical health-related issues. Today's college students communicate far more frequently with their parents than in the past, and while they may not want to talk about sensitive issues like drinking, they often hear what you say and think about it. For many students, their parents' opinions about their behavior still matters.

Given the presence of alcohol in the college social scene, even non-drinkers or those who wait until they are 21 to drink will be exposed to alcohol at some level. They may have a roommate who drinks, get pressured to drink at a party or as part of a group initiation, or find someone in a bathroom who has passed out. Every student needs to be prepared for these situations. So we encourage you to talk with your child early and often about drinking, regardless of whether she or he has ever consumed alcohol.

We recognize that a critical developmental challenge for young adults is navigating the new world of college life without the same direct involvement their parents provided when they were in high school. You can play a vital role in helping them make healthy and responsible choices by providing information, setting expectations, asking questions, and listening to what they have to say. We realize that talking about drinking can be challenging, and what works for one family may not for another. But the stakes are high, and the potential for you to make an impact is real.

It's good to talk about alcohol before your son or daughter leaves for college and also later, after he or she has had a chance to experience college life. Here are a few general suggestions that may be helpful for approaching this topic:

- Approach the issue as a conversation rather than a lecture. Ask your son or daughter what he or she thinks about these issues. Let him or her know that you want to talk about this because you care and want to understand his or her perspective, as well as making sure that he or she understands your views.

- Acknowledge that as a college student, your son or daughter has, or will have, much more independence. Convey that you trust your student, but also that you want to help prepare her or him ahead of time to deal with situations that they are likely to encounter in college.

- Anticipate that your student may react defensively or say that he or she has already learned about this topic in school. You can acknowledge that he or she already knows a lot, but explain that even you are continuing to learn, and you want to make sure he or she has the same understanding of the issues. You can ask for a description of how he or she thinks the social scene is different today from when you were young.

- Think ahead about how you will respond if you are asked about your own use of alcohol when you were young. Some parents choose to say that they won't talk about their own experiences with alcohol because their past is not relevant to the issues facing their child. Others will acknowledge that they drank but note the lessons they learned from their experience or others' about the risks of getting drunk.

- Ask open-ended questions about the social scene to get a sense of what students are experiencing: "What is there to do on campus at night?" "What do your friends like to do for fun?" "Where do people like to hang out?" and "Tell me about your friends." Their responses can set the stage for further conversation about how much drinking they see or think is going on.

While the odds are that your student's time at Cornell will not include serious alcohol-related concerns, a significant number of students do develop problems warranting some level of intervention. (For example, one in 10 students report being concerned he or she has a problem with alcohol or other drugs.) If your son or daughter violates the alcohol- or drug-related rules within the Campus Code of Conduct more than once, our dean of students will contact you to enlist your support. Our aim is to intervene early with education and support services to prevent future incidents and help students who are developing potentially serious problems. In some cases, parents find it difficult to acknowledge that their child has a pattern of heavy drinking. In other situations, our first indication of a problem comes from parents who have noticed a change in their child's behavior, mood, or academic performance. If you have any concerns, please contact the dean of students or the staff at Gannett Health Services' Department of Counseling and Psychological Services for advice.

Navigating the social scene on campus can be challenging for students, and we hope that you will take the opportunity to provide your student with some of the information and tools that can help him or her stay safe and healthy while enjoying the new freedoms and opportunities that college life brings.

FOR MORE INFORMATION

Alcohol-free events: events.cornell.edu

Alcohol and other drug initiatives:
www.gannett.cornell.edu/campus/drugs

Alcohol and other drug services:
www.gannett.cornell.edu/services/counseling/alcohol_drug

Alcohol emergencies and what to do: www.gannett.cornell.edu/
topics/drugs/alcohol/emergencies.cfm

Good Samaritan Protocol: goodsam.cornell.edu

Hazing and alcohol: hazing.cornell.edu

Information about risk reduction and alcohol: www.gannett.cornell.edu/
topics/drugs/alcohol/whattoknow.cfm

"Know the Rules" about alcohol:
www.gannett.cornell.edu/topics/drugs/alcohol/rules.cfm

"Let's Talk," informal confidential consultations with counselors
from Gannett Health Services, with walk-in hours Monday
through Friday at sites around campus:
www.gannett.cornell.edu/services/counseling/caps/talk

Talking about Alcohol

Here are some points that parents and students can discuss during conversations about alcohol and life at college.

- Most Cornell students either don't drink or typically drink in fairly moderate ways. When Cornell students do drink, most tend not to get legally drunk. The ones that do are more noticeable and stand out, which can make it seem like "everybody drinks a lot."

- At Cornell, there are many ways to meet people and have fun other than going to parties with alcohol (even late at night).

- Alcohol is a psychoactive drug that poses considerable risks, as well as potential perceived benefits. When people choose to drink, there are lower-risk and higher-risk ways of doing so.

- Setting a limit before going out and counting one's drinks are ways to reduce risk. A "standard" drink is 12 ounces of beer, 5 ounces of wine, or a shot of alcohol (note that mixed drinks often have far more than a single standard drink).

- Drinking multiple shots or chugging hard alcohol is dangerous and can lead to alcohol poisoning and death.

- "Pre-gaming" shots of alcohol before heading out can get a person drunk quickly and make it more likely that he or she will get sick later.

- If someone is passed out from too much alcohol, it is a medical emergency. Bystanders should call 911 or Gannett Health Services 24/7 if they are not sure the person is sick enough to call for an ambulance. Students should program Gannett's number (607-255-5155) into their phones.

- The law puts safety first. New York law and Cornell's Good Samaritan Protocol take away legal and judicial consequences for possessing and providing alcohol and low-levels of other drugs when someone does the right thing and calls for help.

- Cornell and the Ithaca police enforce New York State's minimum legal drinking age of 21 and the law prohibiting false identification. Our residence halls have even higher standards. Students whose parents express disapproval of underage or dangerous drinking are less likely to engage in those behaviors, so communicating expectations is helpful.

- Being under the influence of alcohol impairs judgment and can lead to risky sexual decisions. It can also decrease a person's ability to resist unwanted sexual contact.

- Students who would never drive drunk are too often willing to ride with a driver who has been drinking, which can be just as dangerous.

- While students know that cars and alcohol don't mix, they also need to know that, at Cornell, walking home at night after drinking can be dangerous because of the gorges on campus. The gorges are remarkable natural areas, but several students have died after falling into them while intoxicated. Students should never stray off the walking paths.

- Having a campus judicial record for certain violations (such as alcohol-related fights) can jeopardize applications to medical school, law school, and government employment.

- Around one in three Cornell students joins one of our many fraternities or sororities, organizations that provide an important sense of connection and friendship for many individuals. At the same time, fraternity and sorority members drink alcohol and experience negative consequences from doing so at twice the level of non-members. While the Cornell community is focused on changing that pattern, it is important to understand both the benefits and risks of being part of these groups.

- The "hazing" of new or current group or team members is a serious problem that often involves coerced drinking. Such activity occurs most frequently in fraternities, sororities, and athletic teams, but it also occurs in other organizations, such as performing arts groups.

KEEP CALM AND LIVE WELL

Mental Health Resources at Cornell

Celia Muoser '13

Celia Muoser '13 (right) with Jamie Tworkowski at To Write Love on Her Arms, an event that is dedicated to presenting hope and finding help for people struggling with depression, addiction, self-injury, and suicide

"The diverse personalities, backgrounds, and interests at Cornell are astounding, and no matter what, you will be able to find someone who is similar to you . . . or someone who is completely different."

As a freshman entering Cornell in the fall of 2009 I could not have imagined how much this school and community would teach me and give to me during my time here. Four years later, as a senior, I knew I was ready to graduate. But at the same time, it was hard to say goodbye to the Cornell campus—I know that it is a place where I will always feel at home.

Although coming to Cornell has been an overwhelmingly positive and defining experience for me, my transition to college was not an easy one. Before college, I had lived in the same small town for most of my life and had gone to school with the same kids since kindergarten. I had never really been on my own before, and I definitely did not anticipate the challenges that I would face transitioning to college and a new community.

Coming to a college where I didn't know anyone was actually much harder than I expected. I had a hard time being apart from my family and boyfriend at the time and also had trouble reaching out to new people and making real connections. I felt incredibly isolated and could not seem to do anything to make it better. Additionally, during my first year there was a string of very public suicides on campus, and for the first time in my life, people who I knew personally were dealing with mental illness.

My first and second semesters at Cornell were very difficult. Though outwardly I presented myself as if I was enjoying all the new experiences, I did not feel like I was really happy about anything. I never thought that I was a person who would have to deal with depression, which is why it took so long for me to realize that something was really wrong. Then, even when I did know something was wrong, I convinced myself that I was too busy with schoolwork and everything else to start seeing a counselor. It wasn't until the summer when I was back at home that I started seeing a therapist and understanding how much my mental state was impacting all areas of my life.

How I felt when I returned to Cornell for my sophomore year was completely different from how I had felt when I left for the summer. I knew that maintaining my well-being was absolutely necessary and needed to come first before anything else. In addition to continuing my counseling at Cornell's Counseling and Psychological Services (CAPS), I started reaching out and connecting with more people. In doing so I realized that all of Cornell had been affected by the suicides the previous year. The concern of the administration, faculty, and students for the well-being of others has shown me the strength of

Left: Cornell Minds Matter Workshops are dedicated to helping students stay in balance by "keeping calm and living well." Topics include building resilience, meditation, self-defense, nutrition and health, overcoming challenges, making time for fitness, journaling for health, and how to help a friend.

"From the moment you step on campus the message that you receive is simple: you are never alone at Cornell."

Cornellians as individuals and, more impressively, of Cornell as a community.

At the beginning of sophomore year I joined a student mental health advocacy group called Cornell Minds Matter (CMM) and immediately became very involved. Through CMM I had the opportunity to be a part of Cornell's efforts to restructure its Mental Health Framework and promote resiliency and help-seeking behavior among students. New initiatives, such as Real Students, Reel Stories (in which all first-year students participate) and Friend 2 Friend were created to help students understand the importance of maintaining the balance among work, school, and play. Resources such as Let's Talk, which provides informal consultations with CAPS counselors at multiple locations around campus, and the Empathy, Assistance, and Referral Service (EARS), a student-run, free and confidential counseling service, were strengthened and publicized. CAPS has increased its counselors and services, and new means restriction measures (on the gorge bridges) are being implemented.

It is vital for everyone to take care of their mental health even if they have not had a personal experience with mental illness. Beginning college can be overwhelming, but at Cornell there are many resources to help new students prepare for and face any obstacles, academic or otherwise, that they may encounter. From the moment you step on campus the message that you receive is simple: you are never alone at Cornell.

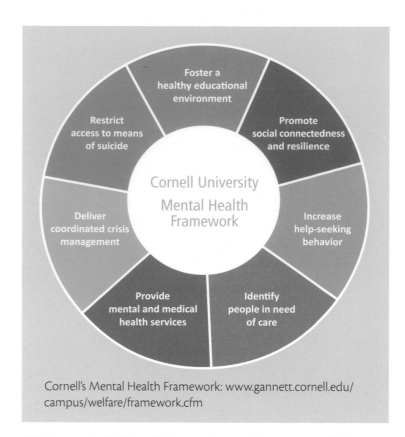

Cornell's Mental Health Framework: www.gannett.cornell.edu/campus/welfare/framework.cfm

Working with CMM and helping others understand mental illnesses and mental health have helped me immensely in working through my own struggles. I feel like I have a true purpose and place on campus because of my involvement with this group. With the knowledge and experience that I have now, there are definitely some things I would have done differently my first year here.

"I have found seeking advice from advisors, professors, and other students very helpful in making both large and small decisions."

Cornell Minds Matter (CMM) students give back to the Ithaca community by volunteering at a mental health day treatment center. CMM has provided community service at Bridges, a home for the elderly; Beverly J. Martin Elementary School; Starlight Mental Health Advocacy Center; Suicide Prevention and Crisis Service; and the local Alzheimer's Association.

A student at the Cornell Minds Matter trip to Buttermilk Falls State Park, one of the 30 social events each semester that aim to get students off campus and enjoy Ithaca

Instead of assuming that others already knew each other or were not looking to make new friends, I would try to make stronger connections during my first semester. I would want to be more involved in extracurricular activities and research my first year, because I really enjoy those things now and feel like I missed out by not participating in them sooner. I would take advantage of Cornell resources such as CAPS, and I would take much better care of my mental health, especially during the transition period from high school to college.

Additionally, I have found seeking advice from advisors, professors, and other students very helpful in making both large and small decisions—you never know who might have insights into your situation. Simply finding an older student in your major who can tell you what certain classes and professors are like can make a huge difference.

The diverse personalities, backgrounds, and interests at Cornell are astounding, and no matter what, you will be able to find someone who is similar to you . . . or someone who is completely different. There is no cookie-cutter Cornell student, and this is one of Cornell's greatest strengths. I have learned that you can only get so far on your own. It is the people around you and your collaboration with others that define your experiences and allow you to succeed. The people that I met at Cornell during my four years as a student have introduced me to many new perspectives, and I hope that I have been able to share some of my own views with them as well.

Pursuing an education at Cornell will not always be easy. There will certainly be challenges inside and outside the classroom, but facing these challenges is an important part of a college education and is paramount in preparing students for the real world after Cornell. Leaving Cornell and going on to medical school, I felt that I was very prepared to succeed in whatever endeavors I undertook in the next few years.

The Cornell community extends far beyond this campus. I knew that I would continue to receive invaluable advice and support from Cornell and other Cornellians even after leaving Ithaca. Though I took away a vast amount of knowledge from my classes, I think I took away even more from the personal connections I made and from the experience of being a part of the community. Sometimes the most important things are not taught in the classroom—as President Skorton once said: "If you learn anything at Cornell, learn to ask for help."

FOR MORE INFORMATION
Cornell University Mental Health Framework:
  www.gannett.cornell.edu/campus/council/framework.cfm
Cornell Minds Matter: mindsmatter.dos.cornell.edu

Dining With Diverse Minds is held twice each semester and enables dialogue and planning among administrators, faculty, staff, and students. Past dinners have addressed alcohol, mental health resources, spirituality, sexual violence, social justice, and creating a caring community at Cornell.

Cornell Minds Matter provides activities at Gratitude Day for students to take a break, relax, and appreciate all they have

Your Student's Mental Health:
What a Parent Can Do

K. Casey Carr '74, assistant dean of students, Cornell University; advisor, Cornell Minds Matter

K. Casey Carr '74

"As a parent, you may be the first to notice
when your student is experiencing difficulty.
You do not have to take on the role of counselor,
you need only notice signs of distress, . . .
express your concern, and offer information
about where he or she can get help."

It was 1976. I had just graduated from Cornell. My sister was finishing up at Queens College when I got a call from my mother . . . "Something is wrong! Your sister has withdrawn from everything; she won't leave her room. Yesterday she burned some old photos and says she can't concentrate on any of her schoolwork. She is crying and saying that there really isn't any reason to live. I don't understand; last month she seemed on top of the world . . . everything was going so well for her and she was so happy." These were the first signs that my sister was developing bipolar disorder. Like with many individuals, her symptoms appeared between the ages of 18 and 24—college age.

It's almost 40 years later. After the start of medication and counseling, my sister did finish college and has a career that she loves. She married and has two lovely daughters both starting out on their own career paths.

As a parent, you may be the first to notice when your student is experiencing difficulty.

You do not have to take on the role of counselor, you need only notice signs of distress, have a supportive conversation with your son or daughter to gather a little more information, reflect your understanding of the difficulties, express your concern, and offer information about where he or she can get help.

All too often, a parent will get a 1 a.m. call from their despondent daughter or son—depressed and tearful, unable to see any solution to a monumental crisis. After a sleepless night, the parents call back only to find that their student has moved on and has no time to talk before getting to their favorite class, going for a run, and then meeting up with friends for dinner.

On the other hand, it is important to identify serious difficulties as early as possible. One of the following indicators alone does not necessarily mean that your student is experiencing distress or mental illness. However, the more indicators you notice over time, the more likely your son or daughter needs some help getting back on track.

Left: Images from Cornell's recently published faculty and staff handbooks: *Recognizing and Responding to Students in Distress* (dos.cornell.edu/faculty_bridge.cfm); its final section, Synopsis of Student Concerns and Conditions, has detailed information about situations that may challenge a student and resources available.

Signs and symptoms

- Missing classes, assignments, or meetings
- Deterioration in quality of work
- Poor concentration, inability to study or do assignments
- Loss of interest and pleasure in others and activities
- Written or artistic expression of violence, despair, or morbidity
- Prolonged depressed or anxious mood, crying spells, or irritability
- Angry hostile outbursts, aggression
- Withdrawn, expressions of hopelessness or worthlessness
- Significant weight loss or gain, decrease in hygiene
- Frequent or chronic illness
- Noticeable cuts, bruises, or burns
- Disorganized speech, confusion
- Bingeing or purging, over exercising
- A gut feeling that something is very wrong
- References to a plan to "end all their problems"

What to do when you are concerned

- Listen carefully and non-judgmentally to your student's situation, thoughts, and feelings. Stay calm even if you are concerned. ("How are things going for you?")
- Allow time for their description of the situation, even if your student has trouble stating what is going on. Allow silences. ("Tell me more about that.")
- Ask open-ended questions that deal directly with the issues in a caring way. ("How are these things affecting your daily life?")
- Point out specific signs you have observed. ("I've noticed lately that you . . . ") And ask for other signs of distress. (Are you finding it difficult to eat, sleep, go to class, get assignments done?")
- Express that you understand and you care. Empathize with your student's feelings and situation, even if they seem exaggerated.
- Restate what you have heard as well as your concern. ("What do you need to do to get back on a healthy path?")
- Ask how you can help.
- Ask what resources your student can use on campus. ("Who is an adult on campus whom you can talk to? What resources are there for you?")
- Suggest resources and referrals.
- The ultimate decision to access resources is the student's. If he or she says, "I'll think about it," it is okay for the moment.
- Keep in touch. Call, text, or Skype again to see how your son or daughter is doing and if (and how) he or she is following up with resources.

- If there are serious signs of a safety risk, ask if they are considering harming themselves. They may be relieved that you asked. Asking the question will not put ideas in their head. (If they say yes, have them call the Gannett Health Services' 24-hour phone line at 607-255-5155 or the crisis service at 607-272-1616.) Check on your student regularly.

Mental illness is a broad descriptive category that can include conditions like major depression, bipolar disorder, anxiety, ADHD, autism, and post-traumatic stress disorder (PTSD). These biological conditions are not the result of personal weakness, lack of character or intelligence, or poor upbringing. Mental illnesses are conditions that arise out of a mix of psychological, social, and biological influences that disrupt a person's thinking, feeling, mood, ability to relate to others, and daily functioning.

The good news is that there are many treatments available today that are very successful. Most people diagnosed with a mental illness can experience relief from their symptoms by actively participating in a treatment plan that often involves a combination of psychotherapy, medication, a healthy lifestyle, and social support.

Some students may need a Health Leave of Absence from Cornell to care for themselves before they continue to pursue their academic path. This often is a very good decision that allows them the time they need to get back in balance and develop resilience skills. A large majority of students who return after a leave of absence report that their remaining time at Cornell is much more productive, focused, and satisfying.

One Student's Experience

As a student, talking to your parents about mental health issues can be extremely hard. On top of the expectations and pressures they consciously or unconsciously place on you, personality differences and the generation gap can make it feel like they couldn't possibly understand the stresses students face daily. For me, the desire to feel independently capable of doing everything made it hard to admit that I was struggling, even to my supportive and loving parents.

When I first reached out to my parents to tell them I wasn't sure if I could finish the semester, they responded with advice and encouragement I couldn't quite hear the way they intended: We know you can figure this out, tell us more about what is going on, your professors might understand if you talk to them . . .

Part of me wanted to curl up in my mom's lap and let her take care of everything, and the other part felt like I had let down anyone who had ever believed in me. It seemed that this was it. I can't do it. I never could. I've failed.

Of course, the real solution lay somewhere in between. I needed to get myself together while letting the resources around me help how they could. But the knowledge of this didn't make it any easier. For nearly a month I sensed impending doom, had restless sleep, lacked focus in class and on work, and withdrew from others. My parents checked in on me and got the number of my roommate to stay updated if necessary. They were still at a distance, but their concern made me want to be able to report good news, and I knew they were there if and when I needed them.

My breaking point came just a couple of weeks before finals. I was no longer functioning. I'd wake up and intend to get dressed but end up back in my bed. I didn't feel like eating and my arms and legs were weak and tingly all over. I was sure I would be kicked out of school, unable to graduate or go anywhere with my life. I have never felt anything close to that kind of anguish. Despite my family telling me they would love me no matter what happened, I felt completely ashamed at my incompetence. With the help of Gannett Health Services, I voluntarily checked into the local psychiatric unit, hoping a change of scene and a break from what my reality had become would help me snap out of this haze.

After a couple of days in the hospital, my dad flew out. He made sure I was well-fed and chased away any doubt that he would do anything to help me through this. The best and the hardest part was that he made sure whatever happened would be my decision. We talked about adulthood and failure and hopes and fears. I learned a lot about my dad in those few days. He went through a lot to get where he is, and he is happy with his life. All the differences between us jumped out at me, but so did the similarities—I inherited not only his nose and curls but also his sense of humor and some portion of his intelligence. After a week, I was feeling better but still wasn't ready to face school. I went home and finished the semester from home, thankful for the accommodations made by the Academic Advising Office and my understanding professors.

The powerlessness I felt did not immediately ease once I got home. I was back in a comforting place, but I began to see things differently than I ever had, questioning everything, terrified of whatever came next. My parents made it clear they would help me in any way they could, but ultimately I had to work at it, too. I began seeing a therapist and my parents helped me structure my days so I wasn't wasting them in bed. Over time, I felt more like myself again. The friends I let in on my struggles were supportive and understood the difficult transitions I was facing, and my parents followed through with their supportive, yet firm, way of helping me figure out what came next.

Back at school after an extended break, I felt so much like the "me" that everyone knew before the breakdown. I'm happy and healthy, but aware that it's possible for me to not be that way if I lose sight of what's important: staying balanced; making time for myself, others, and schoolwork; and knowing what to do if I start spiraling into upsetting thoughts. I feel so lucky to have the Cornell resources and support systems without feeling as though they're being forced on me. I graduated in May, and I am looking forward to the next chapter of my life.

Additional Resources
(All phone numbers are area code 607 and are subject to change.)

For parents:
Don't Tell Me What to Do, Just Send Money: The Essential Parenting Guide to the College Years by Helen Johnson and Christine Schelhas-Miller

For students:
Let's Talk—free, confidential consultations with counselors from Gannett Health Services with walk-in hours at sites around campus Monday–Friday: www.gannett.cornell.edu/services/counseling/caps/talk

Bias/Harassment Concerns: 255-7232

Dean of Students Office: 255-6839

EARS Peer Counseling: 255-3277 (255-EARS)

Gannett Health Services, 24-hour phone consult: 255-5155

International Students and Scholars: 255-5243

Learning Strategies Center: 255-6310

LGBT Resource Center: 254-4987

Religious Affairs: 255-4214

Residential Programs: 255-5533

Student Disability Services: 254-4545

Suicide Crisis Line, 24-hour service: 272-1616

Victim Advocacy: 255-1212

Academic advising services:
Academic Diversity Initiatives: 255-6384

College of Agriculture and Life Sciences: 255-2257

College of Architecture, Art, and Planning: 255-6251

College of Arts and Sciences: 255-5004

College of Engineering: 255-7414

College of Human Ecology: 255-2532

College Veterinary Medicine: 253-3700

Graduate School: 255-7374

Hotel School: 255-6376

ILR School: 255-2223

Johnson: 255-9395

Law School: 255-5839

Office of Internal Transfer: 255-4386

Postdoctoral Studies: 255-5823

Promoting Access Through Universal Design

Kappy Fahey, director, Student Disability Services, Cornell University

Kappy Fahey

"We are working to create a truly inclusive campus that incorporates the philosophy of universal design: the concept that all new environments and programs, to the greatest extent possible, be usable by everyone regardless of their age, ability, or circumstance."

On move-in day in August, I often take the first shift at the Student Disability Services (SDS) table at the Information Fair in Barton Hall. As parents stop by to read our display and brochures, they frequently tell me that there was no such thing as disability services when they were in college. I enjoy having these conversations and sharing some of the rich history of disability services in higher education, where students with disabilities have been at the forefront of opening doors of opportunity and access for many years.

The passage of the Vocational Rehabilitation Act of 1973 was a significant milestone in the history of disability rights for college students. This landmark legislation was fashioned after the Civil Rights Act of 1964 and Title IX of the Education Amendments of 1972, which were based on the concept of equal treatment, or a "color-blind" approach, to end discrimination. The U.S. Congress understood that the goal of equal opportunity was more complex for persons with disabilities. The Federal Register of this law states that "Handicapped persons may require quite different treatment in order to be afforded equal access to federally assisted programs and activities, and identical treatment, in fact, constitutes discrimination."

From this law came the concept of making modifications to policies, practices, and procedures (commonly referred to as reasonable accommodations) to enable students with disabilities to have a level playing field. Then, as now, students with disabilities had to meet established admissions criteria and were required to meet all essential course and program requirements. These are the core principles of disability services in higher education today.

Nationally, 11 percent of all college students self-identify as having a disability. At Cornell, where admissions are selective and students typically attend full time, approximately five percent of our student body (undergraduate, graduate, and professional) self-identify as having a disability.

We are currently experiencing the third significant wave of a student population with disabilities. The first wave occurred after the passage of the Rehabilitation Act of 1973. This group included students with physical and sensory disabilities who had largely been excluded from many college programs because of outright discrimination or because they lacked accessibility.

During the second wave in the 1990s, students with learning disabilities (LD) and attention deficit hyperactivity disorder (ADHD) arrived on college campuses. These students benefited from improved primary and secondary education as a result of the Education for All Handicapped Children Act passed by Congress in 1975 (now called IDEA), which requires special education for all students with

Left: Kaitlin Hardy '12 (front) says her gymnastics coaches, Melanie Dilliplane and Paul Beckwith, helped her regroup after she was sidelined by epilepsy. She is the president and co-founder of FACES, a group that raises epilepsy awareness.

David Feathers, assistant professor of design and environmental analysis, with students in his classroom

"Parents can help by encouraging their son or daughter to be a strong self-advocate and to seek out support systems available at Cornell."

disabilities. Previously, there was little understanding of the nature of learning disabilities and, as a result, generations of students went undiagnosed and were undereducated.

It was easy for many university faculty and staff members to understand the access needs of students with physical disabilities. It was less so for non-obvious disabilities like LD and ADHD. As the faculty saw that students with LD and ADHD could attain the same level of performance and meet academic standards with reasonable accommodations, making those accommodations became routine.

We are currently experiencing a third wave. Students with chronic medical and psychological conditions have increased significantly over the past 10 years. Although in smaller numbers, a new population of students with autism spectrum disorders is significant on college campuses.

In the early days of disability services, the focus was on adapting the individual to the campus environment. Today, much of our focus is on promoting access within the design of a facility, course, or service. At Cornell, we are working to create a truly inclusive campus that incorporates the philosophy of universal design: the concept that all new environments and programs, to the greatest extent possible, be usable by everyone regardless of their age, ability, or circumstance. By applying the principles of universal design at Cornell, we demonstrate that we value the full involvement of all members of our community.

Students and parents often express the concern that using disability services will label them as different or less capable. However, students find that faculty members are quite supportive of the use of disability services. Disability requests are confidential, and the focus of conversations with instructors is on addressing the impact of the condition, not on the condition itself. The SDS office provides letters for students to give to instructors that list the accommodations approved for them. The nature of the disability is not included in the

letters and the student decides which courses require accommodation. There is no record of a student's disability status on a central university database. This information is stored within the SDS office, and records are destroyed five years after a student graduates or leaves the university.

Another concern I hear is that using accommodations is a crutch that will not be available in the real world, so accommodations should not be used in college. Disability services are designed to address the impact of a disability to ensure equal access. And equal access is not an unfair advantage. Accommodations are available and used in the workplace, too. There are quite a few internship and career opportunities for students with disabilities that are designed to facilitate a successful transition from school to work.

I believe that keeping one's condition and accommodation needs to oneself can have a significant negative effect on a student's academic achievement and personal well-being. When students are engaged in addressing the impact of their disability and are empowered to identify workable options to mitigate the impact of a disability, they grow in confidence and feel a greater sense of control about their disability. Parents can help by encouraging their son or daughter to be a strong self-advocate and to seek out support systems available at Cornell.

Cornell students care about the issue of disability access, and there are several disability-related student organizations. The goal of these clubs is to educate about disability issues and create a supportive environment for fellow students. This student activism has had a tremendous positive impact on our campus. In 2010, the Student Assembly (SA) passed a resolution that requires any SA-funded program to use an accessibility checklist when planning its programming. The student organization—Facts, Advocacy, and Control of Epileptic Seizures (FACES)—received grant funding for the first student-led research project on campus. Student activism by the Cornell Union for Disabilities Awareness encouraged more

Sara Furguson '10 founded the Disability Services Troop, a student-run organization, and was its first president

course offerings in disability studies. These courses explore disability laws and policies, design of the environment, and the social construction of (dis)ability in film, literature, and culture. This level of community activism helps to create a welcoming and supportive environment for students with disabilities at Cornell and throughout our community.

Much progress has been made in ensuring accessibility—and by working together, even greater progress will be achieved.

SDS Helped Write My Success Story

Anonymous Cornell alum: R. S. '13

By the second semester of my senior year of college it was hard to believe how quickly my time at Cornell had flown by. During April of my senior year of high school, I visited campus for Cornell Days, an event for admitted students. I vividly remember sitting at an oval table in an office—Student Disability Services (SDS)—on the fourth floor of a building near one of the campus gorges . . . and it was snowing. I was excited to go to Cornell, but nervous about whether my disability would affect my experience there.

While I do not like to label myself as someone with a "disability," I am definitely someone who needed some support and advising from SDS during my time at Cornell. Whether it was for creating the right accommodations, or finding out what documentation I needed to apply for accommodations when taking the MCAT, or seeking advice about how to approach a question with a professor, SDS was always very helpful. I joked to my friends, most of whom had never interacted with SDS, that I was the luckiest student at Cornell because I had the best team of academic, personal, and goal advisors who knew me inside and out.

Being an SDS student at Cornell turned out to be one of the best things about my time on campus. I was always quite capable and adaptable, but excelling at a rigorous academic university with a disability was an incredible building experience. Most of the time, I had no problems—I navigated Cornell just like the rest of my peers. Sometimes, though, I had to make the extra effort to seek some advice or assistance.

I learned to be a great self-advocate. I confidently met with my professors at the beginning of each semester, and my professors got to know me in a way that they don't often get to do with all their students. I explained my challenges, and I knew when to ask for help versus when I could handle things on my own. I learned how to work through my difficulties alongside my professors. I knew when to seek help and how to present my challenges along with my strengths.

It was always reassuring to know that SDS was there to back me up or be a resource to me if I needed. I loved that SDS always asked me how involved it should be. The office knew that I wanted to be my own advocate and that I wanted to work with my professors myself. Before ever emailing or calling a professor, its staff would seek my permission. They respected my decision when I wanted to work by myself, and they were always there to help as soon as I realized that I could use a hand. SDS staff members recognized that I set ambitious goals for myself, and even when I faced challenges, they did all that they could to help me achieve them.

My nerves about entering such a rigorous university while having a disability four years ago seem so far in the past. I held many leadership positions on campus, had academic success, and was accepted to several top graduate schools. My experience as an SDS student at Cornell provided me with the growth and support that I needed to navigate my challenges, my successes, and my future.

FOR MORE INFORMATION
Student Disability Services: sds.cornell.edu

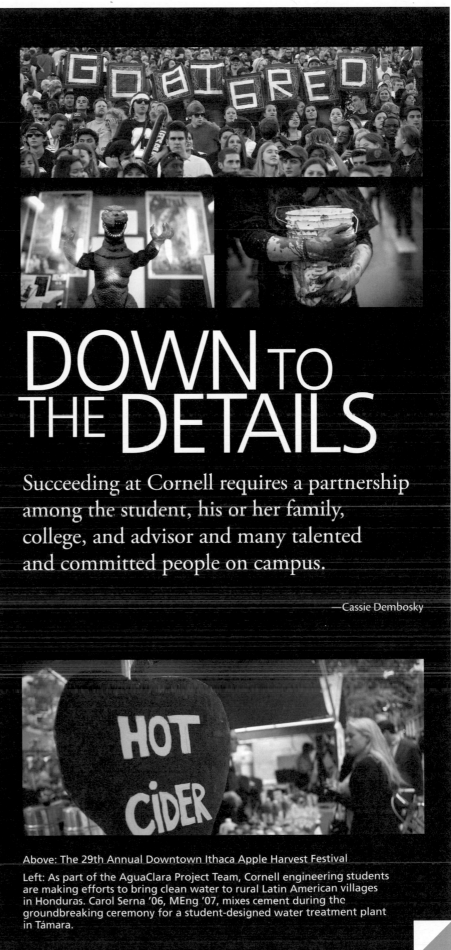

DOWN TO THE DETAILS

Succeeding at Cornell requires a partnership among the student, his or her family, college, and advisor and many talented and committed people on campus.

—Cassie Dembosky

Above: The 29th Annual Downtown Ithaca Apple Harvest Festival

Left: As part of the AguaClara Project Team, Cornell engineering students are making efforts to bring clean water to rural Latin American villages in Honduras. Carol Serna '06, MEng '07, mixes cement during the groundbreaking ceremony for a student-designed water treatment plant in Támara.

Dollars and Sense

Peter E. Olcott, bursar, Cornell University

Peter Olcott

"Our office motto, 'A student is not an interruption of our work, but the purpose of it,' reflects our commitment to provide students and parents with peace of mind and workable financial solutions."

Most families that have sent children off to college have some understanding of the bursar's office, but in general, we are often thought of as that office that sends out bills and wants your money. We are, however, much more than that. The bursar's office provides many services to our students and their families. The term "bursar" originated from the Medieval Latin term *bursarious*, keeper of the purse, or treasurer—but today the term more accurately refers to student financial services.

Our responsibilities include fiscal accountability, customer service, financial counseling, and federal/state reporting—but our overall responsibility is keeping track of a student's financial record (including his or her bursar account, CornellCard account, installment plan, and Cornell-administered loan accounts), collection of those accounts, and working with families to resolve financial issues.

Our office motto, "A student is not an interruption of our work, but the purpose of it," reflects our commitment to provide students and parents with peace of mind and workable financial solutions.

It's important for our students to know and understand their financial responsibilities, as their academics can certainly be affected if their financial house is not in order. One item to remember is that our

office and most Cornell administrative offices, including the registrar and financial aid, conduct business directly with the student. All records and accounts are in the student's name and communications to students are via their Cornell email address. Students and parents should discuss and set expectations for billing, payment, and other bursar issues that need to be addressed.

The bursar's office is considered the central billing office for student charges; almost all charges incurred by a student are posted to his or

Left: Central campus at dusk with views of McGraw Tower and Cayuga Lake

her bursar account from the colleges and units on campus, and those areas retain the detail or back-up information. Our office provides monthly e-billing statements, and bills not paid by the due date incur finance charges.

The bursar e-billing and payment system, Cornell Net.Pay, is online, and students need to be sure they add their parents or other payers, especially those responsible for payment, to their accounts, as we don't provide paper statements. The fall bill is emailed in July and is due in August, and the spring bill is emailed in December and is due in January. The balance due on those statements must be paid by the due date to prevent registration holds. Our office also provides nightly updates to the e-billing system under Recent Activity, so students and families can see transactions and adjustments between billing statements.

Students can also access bursar and CornellCard information via the Student Center website (studentcenter.cornell.edu). The Student Center is only available to students via NetID and password; providing anyone with their NetID and password is a violation of Cornell policy. Our goal is to provide our students and the Cornell community the ability to access information and resolve any issues.

Students can enroll in the CornellCard program, which is an on-campus charge program that allows students to make purchases using their student ID card at places such as the Cornell Store, dining units, athletics, ticket offices, etc. CornellCard is not a debit card—it allows students to charge purchases up to the credit limit of $950, and there is a $12 annual fee for participation. This is a popular service with our undergraduate population, and an added benefit is that it educates our students about credit and the responsible use of it without much risk. The CornellCard account is separate from the bursar account, but is billed on the same monthly statement as the bursar charges. We encourage students and parents to discuss and set expectations for the use of the CornellCard. Some students use it every day to avoid carrying cash, and others use it only for books and supplies or for emergencies.

Jonathan Grey '13, a member of the Cornell men's basketball team

Students and families can enroll in Tuition Pay, also called the Cornell Installment Plan, which allows the balance that is normally due in full for a semester or academic year to be spread out over the course of a semester or academic year. Families set up a budget to cover the amount due and make monthly payments without incurring finance charges, although there is a fee to participate. Once the budget is determined and the plan established, the budget amount for each semester is credited to the student's account and monthly payments are made to the plan to pay off the semester credit. Even though you are on the installment plan, it's important to review your monthly bursar and CornellCard bills, as there may be balances due in addition to your monthly installment payment. Sometimes there is confusion between setting up the installment plan in Tuition Pay and setting up payments in advance with Net.Pay, so be sure you are in the correct module.

Cornell University requires all students to have quality health insurance. It gives the student and their family the peace of mind that comes from knowing you are well-insured. Cornell utilizes a hard waiver system, common on most campuses that have a health insurance requirement, to assure understanding and compliance with this policy: every student is enrolled automatically in Cornell's Student Health Insurance Plan (SHIP). In order to waive enrollment in SHIP, you must demonstrate that you have insurance meeting Cornell's criteria. Detailed information regarding the plan and deadlines for waiving can be found online. The health insurance charge is posted to the student's bursar account in August, unless already waived. A credit will be posted to the bursar account by the student insurance office once a waiver is submitted and approved; the deadline to waive is usually the end of August. Please remember this will need to be done each year that your student is enrolled at Cornell.

The bursar's office and the financial aid office work very closely together, as all financial aid is posted to the student's bursar account. If the aid creates a credit balance, a refund in the student's name is automatically created. Credit balances resulting from cash payments are not refunded until the student requests a refund, and only the student may request a refund. Our preferred method of refunding is via direct deposit, so it is important for students to sign up for direct deposit when they sign up for e-billing. Direct deposit saves students time and money, as they avoid having to pick up and deposit a paper check, and the refund happens much sooner. The bank account must be in the student's name. Joint accounts are fine, but we cannot deposit student refunds to bank accounts that don't have the student name on the account. Information about direct deposit can be found on the bursar website. Please remember: at the time of the refund, not all charges, or recent charges, may be on the account—and the refund will be needed to pay those charges when billed.

"It's important for our students to know and understand their financial responsibilities, as their academics can certainly be affected if their financial house is not in order."

The financial aid office also posts "pending credits" to a student's account, so we may provide the most accurate bill possible and not expect payment for balances that will be covered by financial aid that has been approved but has not yet posted to the account. There are many reasons this might occur. One reason is that federal regulations don't allow us to credit a student's account for federal aid prior to 10 days before class. It may be that your student has an outside scholarship or alternative loan that is in process, or that he or she has not yet completed the entrance interview or signed the master promissory note for his or her student loan.

The bursar statements will include fall pending credits on the July, August, and September statements; the September statement will notify you that fall pending credits will no longer be posted on future bills, and those balances will now be due. The spring pending credits will be included on the December, January, and February statements; the February statement will notify you that spring pending credits will no longer be posted on future bills, and those balances will now be due.

It's important that students review their aid in Student Center and take action to resolve any issues if the pending credits are not resolved by October (for the fall semester) and March (for the spring semester). If not addressed, your student will have a past-due balance and will receive finance charges.

Students enrolled at Cornell may receive an annual 1098-T statement from our office. Alumni who are in repayment on their Cornell-administered loans—such as Federal Perkins, Health Professions, or institutional loans—may also receive a 1098-E statement from Cornell, reporting the interest paid during the calendar year. (Please note: the university will request social security numbers for students who have not provided them, per the 1098-T IRS regulations.) This statement is required by the IRS to report qualified tuition and related expenses; it is an information statement that families may use in determining tax credits or allowances and does not need to be submitted with your tax return. Cornell reports the amount billed on the 1098-T form, not payments made. While our office provides this statement, we are not tax advisors and cannot give tax advice or instruction. We advise you to consult with a tax advisor or review the IRS tax return instructions. Information on this topic is available online, but the student must enroll and then add other users, similar to e-billing enrollment.

Evelyn Ambriz '11 at Miyake Restaurant in Collegetown, working at a part-time job

So, we've shared basic information about the bursar's office—but what are our expectations? Expectations are a two-way street. We expect students and families to be familiar with processes, responsibilities, and due dates—and to contact us as soon as questions or problems arise. And students and families can expect helpful, knowledgeable staff committed to provide outstanding customer service and resolve issues. We strive to respond to inquiries within 24 hours (48 hours during peak times), even if it is to say we are researching the issue and it may take additional time. In addition, students and families should expect our commitment to teaching students life skills and to helping them develop lifelong loyalty and commitment to Cornell, not just in financial support, but in other ways, such as volunteering to help support admissions or to help fundraising efforts.

The Office of the Bursar is always looking to improve its services—please contact us if there is any issue with which we can assist. We hope to encourage and guide students to exercise fiscal responsibility and to be good stewards of their own finances.

FOR MORE INFORMATION

Office of the Bursar: bursar.cornell.edu, uco-bursar@cornell.edu
Cornell Net.Pay: dfa.cornell.edu/treasurer/bursar/studentsparents/paying
CornellCard: dfa.cornell.edu/treasurer/bursar/services/cornellcard
Tuition Pay: dfa.cornell.edu/treasurer/bursar/studentsparents/paying/cip
Student Health Insurance: studentinsurance.cornell.edu
Bursar account direct deposit: dfa.cornell.edu/treasurer/bursar/services/directdeposit.cfm
IRS 1098-T statement and qualified tuition/related expenses: dfa.cornell.edu/treasurer/bursar/studentsparents/tuition/tax.cfm

What Does a Registrar Do?

Cassie Dembosky, registrar, Cornell University

Cassie Dembosky

"Succeeding at Cornell requires a partnership among the student, his or her family, college, and advisor and many talented and committed people on campus."

People ask me all the time, what does the registrar's office do? What does a registrar do?

The Office of the University Registrar provides so many services. First and foremost, the university registrar is charged with protecting a student's academic record by enforcing federal law and university policy. We also support class enrollment and grading. We create and distribute transcripts, diplomas, and university ID cards, and we build the university's Courses of Study (courses.cornell.edu), class schedule, and final exam schedule.

The Family Educational Rights and Privacy Act (FERPA) was enacted in 1972. Its purpose is twofold: to protect a student's educational record by preventing unauthorized access; and, to provide a student the opportunity to review and, if they deem necessary, request an amendment to their record.

All current students and alumni have the right to:

- inspect and review their education records

- consent to disclosures of personally identifiable information contained in their education records

- request the amendment of their education record if they believe it is inaccurate

Chiming bells atop McGraw Tower

- file a complaint with the U.S. Department of Education concerning alleged failures by Cornell University to comply with the requirements of FERPA

FERPA allows institutions to implement the law with a fair amount of flexibility. You'll find that Cornell's interpretation is conservative. We make information available to university officials who need access for legitimate business needs, but in general, we don't provide information to a student's parents or guardians.

Left: Costumed revelers at Dragon Day

When we feel it is in the best interest of your student, we will contact you, especially if we feel the student's status at the university is in jeopardy. In addition, parents or guardians may be contacted when:

- a student has voluntarily withdrawn from the university or has been required by the university to withdraw

- a student has been placed on academic warning

- a student's academic good standing or promotion is at issue

- a student engages in alcohol- or drug-related behavior that violates Cornell policies

- a student has been placed on disciplinary probation or restriction

- in exceptional cases, a student otherwise engages in behavior calling into question the appropriateness of his or her continued enrollment in the university

There are two very important pieces of FERPA that all families and students need to understand. First, some student information is considered public-eligible—it's called directory information. Included is the student's name, local and cell telephone numbers, email address, photograph, major field of study and college attended, academic level, dates of attendance, enrollment status, participation in officially recognized activities and sports, weight and height (of members of athletic teams), and any degrees earned and awards received. Cornell may make this information public. For example, it might be published in the online directory, shared with a scholarship benefactor, or provided to various agencies (such as insurance agencies) that need to verify enrollment. Students may opt to suppress access to their directory information. If they do so, the information will not be released without the student's written permission.

"Please remind your student to keep personal information up to date in the university system. Using Student Center, students can update many items, including home address, cellphone number, emergency contact information, and emergency notification information."

A second important concept related to FERPA is that Cornell will not release a student's non-directory information without his or her written permission. The student needs to provide consent for each disclosure. Students are adults, and they have the responsibility and right to protect their information. We expect your student to work with you when it comes to enrollment and grades. If you want to see grades, ask your student to share them. It will promote a great dialog about their progress, classes they are thriving in, and areas where they need a bit of help and encouragement.

Beyond FERPA, my office supports a variety of information systems that enable students to enroll in classes, look up course descriptions, determine when classes meet and when exams will be held, and order transcripts. The systems enable faculty to submit grades and academic advisors to learn more about their students' classes and academic progress.

There are many administrative offices your student will likely need to become familiar with—the Office of Financial Aid and Student Employment, the Office of the University Bursar, and his or her college's registrar and student service offices. College registrar offices are responsible for maintaining the student's record, tracking progress toward a degree, and, in some cases, academic advising.

Students use an online tool called Student Center (studentcenter. cornell.edu) to accomplish much of their administrative work. Using Student Center, they will enroll in their classes during the pre-enrollment and add/drop periods. Midway through each semester, students pre-enroll in their classes for the upcoming semester. Add/drop begins just prior to the start of the semester, and at that time students can make changes to their schedules by adding new courses, swapping existing ones, and dropping courses that don't quite fit.

Before any enrollment begins, your student should meet with his or her advisor and begin to plot out a curriculum for the upcoming semesters. Your son or daughter also needs to talk with you. Help him or her figure out interests and goals—and encourage your student to explore disciplines he or she didn't even know existed or to try classes that will challenge the way he or she thinks. When it comes down to actually enrolling in the classes, your student must do it. Student Center is password protected; only the student may log in, and only the student can enroll in classes. (It's a violation of Cornell University policy to share passwords.)

Speaking of enrolling in classes, please don't fret if your student does not immediately get into her or his required or first-choice classes. Cornell offers more than 5,000 courses. There's so much to choose from—a second-choice course could provide an exciting opportunity to explore something new. If your student isn't able to enroll in a required class during the enrollment periods, she or he needs to talk with an advisor and contact her or his college's registrar's office.

Stephen Breedon '14, a student in the School of Hotel Administration, catches up with friends

No student has ever graduated from Cornell without having taken all required courses! They may not successfully enroll in the class within the first few minutes of the enrollment period, but they will get in.

Please remind your student to keep personal information up to date in the university system. Using Student Center, students can update many items, including home address, cellphone number, emergency contact information, and emergency notification information. All of this information is critically important to the university in the event of an emergency. It is also used to communicate about various events and opportunities such as First-Year Parents' Weekend and Commencement.

Also in Student Center, students can view their registration status. University registration is the official recognition of a student's relationship with the university and is the basic authorization for a student's access to services and education. To be registered, a student must:

- settle all financial accounts, including current semester tuition

- satisfy New York State and university health requirements

- have no holds from their college, the Office of the Judicial Administrator, Gannett Health Services, or the bursar

At the beginning of each semester, students receive an email message from me that asks them to check Student Center for holds that are preventing registration. The absence of holds means the student has met the requirements and is registered. If there are registration holds, they must be cleared by the end of the third week of classes. To have a hold cleared, your student needs to work with the office that placed the hold. If a student becomes registered after the end of the third week of classes, they are assessed a late fee of at least $350. Students who fail to register by the deadline risk being withdrawn from the university.

Cornell does not send grade reports to students (or their families). Students can view their final grades in Student Center. They can also request official transcripts. Cornell offers traditional paper transcripts as well as e-transcripts (which are delivered electronically as secure and signed pdf documents). If you wish to receive your student's transcript, ask your student to request one for you. E-transcripts are delivered within minutes.

Much of your student's experience will be in the classroom, library, and laboratory. Please also encourage your son or daughter to do things outside the classroom—get involved in community service, extracurricular activities, or sports; go to movies and concerts; take in a lacrosse game; or just relax on the Arts Quad. And please encourage them to eat well, get enough sleep, and have fun!

Succeeding at Cornell requires a partnership among the student, his or her family, college, and advisor and many talented and committed people on campus. It's a wonderful experience.

Welcome to the Cornell family!

The operations research and information engineering undergraduate graduation ceremony

FOR MORE INFORMATION
Office of the University Registrar: registrar.sas.cornell.edu
Courses of Study: courses.cornell.edu
College registrar directory:
    registrar.sas.cornell.edu/Student/crdirectory.html
Cornell policies important to students: policy.cornell.edu
    Search in "Policy Volumes" for:
    Policy 4.5 Access to Student Information
    Policy 5.1 Responsible Use of Information Technology Resources
    Policy 5.8 Authentication to IT Resources
    Policy 5.10 Information Security

Cornell's Perspective on Financial Aid

Thomas Keane, director, financial aid, Office of Financial Aid and Student Employment

Thomas Keane

"I believe that our policy helps to achieve a public good: leveling the cost of Cornell across economic classes."

In my position, I have the privilege of overseeing the development and implementation of Cornell's need-based financial aid policy for undergraduate students. In summing up our policy, I often use the phrase: "helping students who could not otherwise afford to attend."

To me, this is a powerful statement—it represents one of Cornell's most noble goals: to provide the opportunity to study at a world-class institution. Cornell is an expensive university with highly selective admissions, and it produces graduates who work around the world. I believe that our policy helps to achieve a public good: leveling the cost of Cornell across economic classes. Armed with a Cornell degree, our undergraduates are represented in so many graduate schools, professions, and volunteer activities—they're too numerous to count.

Helping to provide this educational opportunity to those students whose families cannot afford to pay the full bill on their own is an awesome responsibility. Meeting that responsibility requires a delicate balancing act on the part of the financial aid professional; in some ways, a split personality. On one hand, we attempt to provide enough assistance to enable students to decide to enroll at Cornell without

Students and faculty from the School of Operations Research and Information Engineering in the College of Engineering

taking on a crushing level of paid work or indebtedness. On the other hand, we need to preserve the university's resources so that we can maximize teaching, research, and service efforts. The split personality aspect of our role can make for some difficult decisions over the course of time.

In order to accomplish our mission, we require application forms, tax returns, supplemental verification forms, certification statements,

We provide opportunities for students to study abroad as part of the undergraduate experience, adjust aid packages as family financial circumstances change, and obtain funding for non-standard educational expenses such as computer purchases, special course supplies, and Cornell student health insurance premiums.

documentation of financial affairs—and we may need to ask (sometimes uncomfortable) questions of students and families. All of this is needed to satisfy the trustees of the university, our students, and their families as we assess each applicant equitably and consistently. We take on this role with all appropriate seriousness and expect that students and families will as well.

Financial aid at Cornell encompasses any type of financial assistance we provide to help the student meet his or her financial obligations while pursuing an undergraduate degree program. The financial assistance can be a job, a loan, a grant, or a scholarship (we use the terms "grant" and "scholarship" interchangeably). Jobs require work for pay and might be funded by the university alone or in combination with a federal aid program called Federal Work Study. Loans require a promise to repay in the form of an electronic signature on a "promissory note" and are mostly funded by the federal aid programs in the Federal Direct Loan program or the Perkins Loan program. Grants or scholarships provide money that does not need to be repaid and usually have no requirements other than to pursue your degree and maintain satisfactory performance. Grants and scholarships are provided by the university directly or from gifts made by alumni and friends of the university, the federal and state governments, and private agencies.

While Cornell depends on state and federal assistance, the vast majority of financial assistance for students comes from the university itself. Meeting the needs of state and federal regulations, as well as Cornell policies and procedures can be a daunting task. Please know that we try to keep processes as simple as possible while also protecting you and the university from fraud and abuse. You can help by learning about and meeting deadlines, providing all aid application documents when requested, being honest, and by asking questions when you don't understand our policies or procedures.

Along with our primary mission, we also provide opportunities for students to study abroad as part of the undergraduate experience, adjust aid packages as family financial circumstances change, and obtain funding for non-standard educational expenses such as computer purchases, special course supplies (such as art and photography), and Cornell student health insurance premiums.

Finally, unlike admissions, financial aid is an every-year process. While we do our best to keep the family contribution component of the aid package consistent from year to year, there are always changes in programs, so ask your son or daughter to be mindful of re-application deadlines (traditionally late April or early May) and news about the re-application process.

FOR MORE INFORMATION
Financial Aid office: finaid@cornell.edu
The best way to connect is by visiting and meeting with one of our financial aid counselors. See www.finaid.cornell.edu.

Tips to Help your Son or Daughter Succeed With Finances

• **Help plan finances in advance.**
Your student is a partner in the financing plan. Create a budget plan, then monitor and adjust the plan as needed. While parents play a big role in financing, the ultimate responsibility remains with the student as both the degree and the bill will be in his or her name.

• **Review the bill.**
Make sure you and your son or daughter review the monthly bill from the bursar (our student account office). Are the charges correct, is all the aid showing up as credits, are all your payments reflected on the account?

• **Limit your loans and personal debt to the essentials.**
When used wisely, loans are an excellent tool to help you reach your educational goals. Credit cards can be useful to manage cash flow shortages or emergencies but can be a nightmare when used to finance things you can't really afford.

• **Contact us if your family's circumstances change.**
We can make a mid-year adjustment if something significant has occurred, such as loss of employment or illness of a parent.

• **Re-apply on time.**
Missed deadlines can delay your student's return to school.

• **Be accurate and honest.**
Accuracy in completing the aid application will yield the best results for your family. Honesty will keep you from running into problems with our fraud and financial irregularity policies.

• **Ask for help when you need it.**
Helping people is why most of us started in the business.

The Role of the Judicial Administrator

Mary Beth Grant, judicial administrator, Cornell University

Mary Beth Grant

"I always treat each student as I would want one of my own children to be treated . . . Ultimately, the campus disciplinary process serves to support the education that students receive in the classroom."

When people learn about the type of work I do at Cornell, they often reflect, "Oh, so you work with the bad kids!" I quickly disabuse them of this notion by explaining that I work with good students who have made bad choices. Students, like all human beings, make mistakes. Since undergraduates are late adolescents and their frontal lobes are not fully developed, they do not have judgment that is fully developed. The role of Cornell's campus disciplinary system is to help these students learn from their mistakes by holding them accountable and to make sure the educational environment for the rest of the community is not negatively impacted by these mistakes.

One of the most important things I have learned during my 14 years as judicial administrator (or, to use the vernacular, JA) is that conflict leads to growth. When a student engages in conduct that violates the Code of Conduct, and when the campus disciplinary system holds that student accountable, the student experiences conflict: no one likes to be confronted for misbehavior. But, the conflict creates a space for the student to reflect on his or her values and the values of Cornell's community and to consider whether his or her behavior matched those values. This reflection allows students to struggle, to learn, and to grow.

The entrance to Day Hall, the university's administrative building, covered in fall ivy

This philosophy applies in cases that are considered more minor and those that are extremely serious. For example, when a student is confronted with his or her consumption of alcohol when he or she is not 21 years old, the student sometimes has to reconcile that the values of peers may not be the values of the institution. The student will have an opportunity to learn more about safety and, in the process, will learn that among Cornell students who drink, the vast majority consumes alcohol in safe ways. The student will struggle with the myths and the facts—learning that "everyone does it" is not a good excuse, nor is it true. And, the student will be better able to assess risks of his or her behavior. If the value of alcohol consumption exceeds the value of participating in a Cornell education, it should raise concerns both for the student and the family.

Students sometimes have a harder time understanding the educational philosophy in serious cases; for example, when a student engages in an act of violence that will certainly result in a separation from Cornell. For accused students, the "educational" approach might feel punitive because their education is being interrupted. For complainants, victims of the violence, the "educational" approach might not feel punitive enough because this system cannot put someone in jail, nor eliminate the trauma experienced by the complainant. Yet, the philosophy does still apply. Holding the accused person accountable for serious misconduct affords him or her the knowledge that he or she has the capacity to act in ways that deviate significantly from the values of self, family, and community and provides the opportunity to reflect on that information. Often these cases are fueled by alcohol, peer pressure, or a lack of understanding of the rules. Being held accountable creates a learning experience that differs significantly from the bravado that may accompany escaping consequences.

Additionally, for both minor and serious cases, the education of the rest of the community must be considered. In serious cases, there are often complainants whose education has been negatively impacted by the accused. Addressing this in ways to remediate this disruption is a critical part of honoring the values of the code. The entire Cornell University community can be impacted by both minor and serious misconduct. To carry through the example of underage drinking, residence hall communities are impacted by bathrooms covered in vomit or by noisy, disruptive, intoxicated residents; Greek houses lose the respect their philanthropic works engender if their members act like *Animal House*; and Ithaca's permanent residents may miss the energy and enthusiasm of living in a college community if some students misrepresent the norm of student behavior by trashing community property.

For students who are complainants, victims of another's misconduct, it is important to know that the JA's office provides information about resources that can help the complainant through the trauma. In particular, the victim's advocate can help navigate the various systems and services through Counseling and Psychological Services and can assist a complainant with the strong emotions that may accompany a negative situation. While the JA cannot guarantee any particular outcome for a complaint, the complainant will be encouraged to share his or her feelings about the appropriate resolution and has some appeal rights if the case does not come out the way she or he anticipated. Additionally, and significantly, the complainant will be provided information about how to contact the police if the complainant wishes to file a criminal complaint in addition to

the campus complaint. While the JA encourages complainants to pursue both a criminal complaint and a campus complaint, it is up to the victim to decide in which arena he or she wishes to proceed.

As family members of Cornell students, it is important for you to know that the processes in the campus disciplinary system are fair, that all parties have the right to be fully heard, and the members of the community involved in the system work hard to carefully evaluate all the information about every case. Whether it is a member of the JA's office, a board chair, or board members, each person works hard both to understand the facts to determine if there is a code violation and to evaluate the appropriate sanction. I always treat each student as I would want one of my own children to be treated, (and as I am a parent of two college-aged children, this is significant).

Ultimately, the campus disciplinary process serves to support the education that students receive in the classroom. By addressing disruptions to the educational environment and by challenging accused students to live up to their values and those of the community, students have a broader education and are better able to make appropriate judgments in the future.

FOR MORE INFORMATION
Campus Judicial System: judicialadministrator.cornell.edu
Campus Code of Conduct: dfa.cornell.edu/treasurer/policyoffice/
    policies/volumes/governance/campuscode.cfm
Title IX: share.cornell.edu/policies-laws

Our Primary Responsibility: Keeping Your Student Safe

Kathy Zoner, chief, Cornell University Police

Kathy Zoner (back, right) and her family

"My hope for all Cornell students is that they embrace the wide variety of different cultures that exist at the university . . . Cornell is abundant with life, and opportunity is there just for the taking."

Cornell is a wonderful institution where people both young and old can study, grow, and mature—and it's a great place to work. It has been my privilege to serve the Cornell community as a member of the Cornell University Police Department for the past 21 years, including the last three years as chief of the department. As one of our former officers often said: "We view our job here as making Cornell a place where I would love to send my child."

People must feel safe in order to maximize the benefit of their experience here, so a big part of our job is making sure the university community knows that we're here for them. A university police department is not just a law enforcement agency in the sense of a local police or sheriff's department. We operate in a culture that is more nuanced and gray—it's not only a stark, black-and-white question of whether or not someone has violated the law.

For example, the annual Dragon Day in March is a university tradition more than a century old. Over time, the tradition began to attract local schoolteachers, who would bring their elementary and middle school classes to campus to view the celebration.

Dragon Day 2012

Unfortunately, earlier incarnations of the parade often turned into rowdy affairs with students getting drunk and making poor decisions. Visitors to campus found themselves in the paths of various projectiles thrown about by students.

The Dragon Day parade, which was started by architecture students, deteriorated so much that the College of Architecture, Art, and Planning cut ties with the event. The Cornell Police worked with the school not to stop the parade but to really make it a parade again.

Studying late at the library? Walking home after dark? Catch a free ride with BLUE, a shuttle service that picks you up on campus and brings you directly to your doorstep.

Yes, according to tradition, there would be a confrontation of some kind between students from Architecture, Art, and Planning and the College of Engineering. However, the good-natured confrontation now takes place within the rules and boundaries established by the deans of the colleges and Cornell Police with input from the student groups who stage the event. Cornell Police encourages students to participate in the many activities available to them but in a safe manner for all.

The safety of the university community is our primary responsibility, and during my time at Cornell, one of the issues that keeps resurfacing is how much alcohol and drug abuse are a detriment to this educational environment as a whole. Alcohol and drug use and abuse cause injury and illness and inhibit a student's capacity to thrive.

When they arrive at Cornell, most new students may project the appearance of adulthood because of their age and physical maturity, and yet, for the most part, they lack the life experience that would allow them to routinely make good decisions in order to safely stand on their own two feet. Alcohol and drugs can lead people to make poor decisions that all too often hurt them or somebody else. Sometimes those decisions end in death; calling parents to tell them their child has been severely injured (or worse) is a heart-breaking part of our duties.

As a parent of three small children, I often think of the day when they will leave home. Wherever they end up attending college, there are questions I will want answered before my son or daughter enrolls. One of the first things I would do is visit a university's counseling center and law enforcement agency to see for myself their capacity to deal with high-stress situations and if they understand the type

of journey a young person takes at this point in their life. I would want to feel that my child is as safe as possible in the environment to which I'm sending them alone, perhaps for the first time, for an extended period.

Before your child enrolls at a college you may ask to see the institution's annual crime report, usually available online at the college's website. Required by federal law, the annual report (often called the Clery report) offers statistical information about violent crimes and drug offenses. Also readily available in this same report are the institution's policy statements on safety matters. The Clery report doesn't include the more pervasive property crimes, so you should also inquire about the data regarding incidences of damage to and theft of property in order to get a more comprehensive feel for the safety of the institution's environment.

My hope for all Cornell students is that they embrace the wide variety of different cultures that exist at the university and take full advantage of the opportunities for social growth while receiving a great education. Cornell is abundant with life, and opportunity is there just for the taking.

My advice to new students is to come to Cornell with their eyes and ears open. To get the most from their educational experience, they must remain open to the idea that much of their education will take place away from the classroom. I remind them to practice the Golden Rule: treat others the way they want to be treated and respect the personal property of others. I advise students to always act as a concerned citizen, if not a close friend, during their time here. For example, if someone is inebriated to the point where he or she can't take care of him or herself, don't just walk away. Students should become familiar with support services on campus before they need them. Many resources are available to help with problems from the little "leg up" to the "catch me, I'm falling" levels of assistance. Early intervention is key to success.

> "I advise students to always act as a concerned citizen, if not a close friend, during their time here."

The Cornell Police, like other university staff, care deeply about our students and want each of them to achieve his or her potential in the best environment possible. Our ultimate goal is keeping our students safe. If students' actions are making themselves or others less safe, we must, and will, step in. If students find themselves lost, needing assistance in finding resources, or simply wanting to know what is available to help keep them safe, we are centrally located in Barton Hall or just a phone call away—24 hours a day, 7 days a week, 365 days a year—to provide guidance and support.

FOR MORE INFORMATION
Cornell University Police: cupolice.cornell.edu, 607-255-1111

A Guide to Computing at Cornell

Ted Dodds, chief information officer and vice president, information technologies, Cornell University

Ted Dodds

"Cornell provides many resources to help students strengthen their core academic skills in finding, evaluating, sharing, and creating content using information technologies and the Internet."

Online resources for students at Cornell are provided centrally and at the college level. A good starting point is the IT@Cornell student's page.

it.cornell.edu/for/students.cfm

Wi-Fi and Wired Connections

All residence halls provide Internet connectivity for students. Most residence hall rooms have both Wi-Fi and wired network connections. Cornell also provides Wi-Fi service in key public spaces throughout the campus, including libraries, student study lounges, and many campus dining facilities and academic buildings. Secure, standard, and guest access options are offered.

Usage of on-campus network resources is unlimited. For off-campus network resources, students have a limit of 100 gigabytes (GB) of data transfer per month (most students never exceed this limit). Usage that exceeds 100 GB in a month is billed at the rate of $0.0015 per additional megabyte (MB).

it.cornell.edu/services/guides/getting_connected

Cornell NetIDs

Each student is assigned a personal, unique identifier called a Network ID (or NetID). It consists of the student's initials followed by one or more numbers (for example, ewe1). Students use their NetID, along with a password, to obtain secure access to online services at Cornell.

NetIDs are for students' exclusive personal use. It is a violation of university policy to share a NetID password with anyone, including family members.

it.cornell.edu/services/netid

Email

Cornell students receive an email address in the form of "NetID@cornell.edu" and a 25-gigabyte account on Cmail (powered by Google Apps for Education). Students can choose to use Cmail and/or provide a valid, alternate email address where their Cornell email will be forwarded. Along with email, Cmail includes calendar, collaboration, and other tools.

it.cornell.edu/services/guides/student_email

Student Center

Students can review their grades, check their registration status, enroll in courses, request a transcript, see their financial information, and update their home/local addresses and emergency contact information through Cornell's Student Center.

registrar.sas.cornell.edu/student/studentcenter.html

Help with Online Resources

For questions or concerns about using Cornell's online resources, students can contact the IT Service Desk by email, phone, chat, or in person.

it.cornell.edu/catc/cms/support/index.cfm

They can also search and browse through extensive self-help online resources on the IT@Cornell website.

it.cornell.edu/support/online.cfm

Computers and Accessories

Cornell does not require students to own a computer, but many students prefer the convenience of having one. The Cornell Store's Technology Connection offers computer equipment from several manufacturers to the Cornell community at academic discount prices. In addition to computers, they also offer software, accessories, computer service, and books on computing.

store.cornell.edu/t-new-students.aspx

Secure Computing

All students are expected to keep their computer secure while it's connected to the Cornell networks. The university also provides guidance on how to guard against fraud and protect privacy. Encourage your student to learn about the steps he or she needs to take.

it.cornell.edu/security/students.cfm

Copyright and Responsible Use of IT Resources

Citizenship rights and obligations are central to the education we provide students about the appropriate use of IT resources. That education begins with the understanding that anything illegal or a violation of policy in physical space applies to the Internet, as well. This is particularly true when it comes to distributing content for which the student does not hold the copyright or the license to distribute—whether via file-sharing programs (songs, movies, television shows, gaming software) or campus Intranet (homework assignments, papers, instructor manuals) used in violation of Cornell's Academic Integrity policy. Social norms, the market, and law are in flux during times of rapid technological change—as part of our IT education, we encourage our students to work toward lawful solutions to technology challenges.

it.cornell.edu/policies/copyright/index.cfm

Software

Many new students ask what sort of software they will need. Beyond a word processing program and antivirus software (available for free from Cornell), it really depends on the student's field of study. CU Software Licensing Services serves the Cornell community as a resource for software pricing and core applications used by students.

Much of the software used in courses is provided in the. If needed software is not available in the labs, students should be able to purchase it at the Cornell Store (store.cornell.edu).

it.cornell.edu/services/software_licensing

Printing

Students can use low-cost, black-and-white and color laser printers located throughout the campus. With Cornell's Net-Print service, students can print from a computer lab or their own computer.

it.cornell.edu/services/netprint

Repair Services

Through a partnership with a locally owned business, the Cornell Store's Technology Connection arranges for authorized, warranty repair service for Apple, Dell, Hewlett Packard, and other manufacturers and also offers data recovery.

store.cornell.edu/c-556-repairs.aspx

Computer Labs

Students can use Cornell's online resources and work on assignments in computer labs around campus. The labs have Windows and Macintosh computers, a variety of software, and networked laser printers.

cit.cornell.edu/services/labs

Blackboard

For many courses, Cornell students use Blackboard to access online course materials, including assignments, notes, discussion forums, slideshows, quizzes, and more.

it.cornell.edu/services/blackboard/studentguide

File Storage

Cornell Box gives each student 10 gigabytes of online storage, with options to collaborate on documents in real time and share access to files instantly.

it.cornell.edu/services/box

Digital Literacy

Cornell provides many resources to help students strengthen their core academic skills in finding, evaluating, sharing, and creating content using information technologies and the Internet. Students can take advantage of self-guided web resources, instructor-led workshops, and multiple library-based services.

digitalliteracy.cornell.edu

LOOKING AHEAD

Cornell's dazzling array of opportunities will help your student write his or her score. While this will include academic studies and a choice of major, your student's manuscript will be highlighted by friendships, clubs, roommates, and living choices and will be punctuated by memories, contributions, and achievements. As you hug your son or daughter before leaving campus, know this is a time he or she will make his or her own way, take risks, set goals, and stretch personal boundaries!

—Jeff Weiss '79

Left: Leo Villareal's *Cosmos* light installation, an exhibition at the Johnson Museum of Art; courtesy of the Johnson Museum of Art (photo: James Ewing)

Considering Graduate and Professional Schools

Barbara A. Knuth, vice provost, Cornell University; dean, Graduate School; professor, Department of Natural Resources, College of Agriculture and Life Sciences

Barbara Knuth

"The most successful graduate and professional students are those who are completing further education through their own drive, ambition, and self-articulated career goals."

It's not too early to support your son or daughter in thinking about what's next after his or her Cornell undergraduate education. According to the postgraduate survey conducted annually by Cornell Career Services, about one third of Cornell bachelor's degree recipients go on to graduate or professional school immediately after graduation. Over the next few years, and typically within the first six years after graduation, almost three quarters of Cornell's undergraduate alumni will continue their education in some way through research-oriented graduate studies or professional studies in engineering, law, medicine, health careers, business, management, or other fields.

Earning a graduate or professional degree provides an opportunity for your daughter or son to explore her or his personal interests and passions in depth after receiving a bachelor's degree, helps develop a particular set of skills, opens up additional career paths, and often leads to increased earning power over the course of a career. You can start helping your Cornell student prepare for this next educational stage in his or her life now.

Most graduate and professional schools consider a variety of criteria in making admissions decisions, including a student's overall academic record as an undergraduate. But many will focus on the achievement in particular courses or areas of study that most closely relate to the likely emphasis in graduate or professional studies. Encourage your son or daughter to explore Cornell courses widely. It will help in the discovery of his or her own intellectual and professional passions that he or she may want to focus on in more depth in graduate or professional schools and into a career, and it will help identify where and how your student might want to have an impact in the world.

In addition to his or her courses, there are a multitude of other opportunities available for your student at Cornell University—a world-class research institution. Cornell faculty and graduate students are eager to work with undergraduates as members of their research teams, and undergraduates, in turn, learn about the research enterprise, develop marvelous mentoring relationships with graduate students and faculty, and hone their own intellectual interests. This hands-on experience helps undergraduates consider whether a research path is right for them. A research-oriented career can be both collaborative and team focused as well as very independent and entrepreneurial. Students considering research graduate studies should test out different types of research opportunities at Cornell—in the lab, in the field, in the library, and even abroad—to see if the creativity and independence of a research-based career appeals to them. Most importantly, working side by side with graduate student and faculty researchers will give

Left: Hojoong Kwak, a graduate student in molecular biology and genetics, studying eukaryotic transcription

your son or daughter insights about the lifestyle and commitment required to be successful in graduate school.

Many application processes require certain standard examinations, such as the GRE for graduate schools, the MCAT for medical schools, the GMAT for business schools, or the LSAT for law schools. Look into these exams with your student, so you both know what they require, and support your son or daughter in preparing for them. Numerous preparation handbooks and courses are available for most of these types of exams; most importantly, you can motivate your student to take the time to study and prepare seriously for these exams independently or with the help of support groups.

Recommendations from faculty are particularly important for graduate school admissions. Encourage your son or daughter to make an effort, each semester, to get to know at least one faculty member who would be well positioned to write a positive, insightful recommendation. Working in a faculty member's research program is one way to build this relationship, but your student can also attend office hours held by his or her teachers, interact with faculty-in-residence or faculty fellows (on North Campus) or house professors (on West Campus), or get to know the faculty advisors for the student group in which she or he participates.

Pursuing graduate or professional studies can be two very different experiences. Typically, pursuing graduate studies toward a research degree (such as a master of science or a PhD) requires finding both a university and a faculty member mentor that are good fits for the

> "Encourage your son or daughter to make an effort, each semester, to get to know at least one faculty member who would be well positioned to write a positive, insightful recommendation."

student, given the highly personalized nature of the research mentorship relationship. Often PhD students are provided sufficient funding through a stipend and tuition award so that the school they attend largely covers their educational expenses. Working toward a professional degree typically requires comparatively more financial investment from the student and may not be as individualized as a research degree program.

The most successful graduate and professional students are those who are completing further education through their own drive, ambition, and self-articulated career goals. Students should understand that having a sense of what they want to be doing in the future is critical in informing their choice of the appropriate graduate or professional school at which to continue their education. It's fine to take time off between undergraduate and graduate school experiences. Whether his or her career interests are in higher education, industry, government, business, healthcare, law, or nonprofits, graduate or professional education is likely in your student's future. Support your son or daughter in exploring the possibilities.

Stephanie Delgado, Cornell Law School Class of 2014, studies in the Law Library

Michael-Paul Robinson, a graduate student in chemical and biomolecular engineering, works in an Olin Hall Lab

Chioma Enweasor,
Weill Cornell Medical College
Class of 2016

Ben Tettlebaum '12 came to
Cornell Law School to find an
intellectual challenge, a different
sort of lifestyle, and a new way to
create positive change

Arthur Soroken, MBA student at
the Samuel Curtis Johnson
Graduate School of Management
at Cornell University

Nasim Khadem '08, MD '12
received a Doctor of Medicine
with Honors in Service from
Weill Cornell Medical College

FOR MORE INFORMATION
GRE: ets.org/gre
GMAT: mba.com/the-gmat
MCAT: aamc.org/mcat
LSAT: lsac.org/jd/lsat/about-the-lsat.asp
Cornell Career Services: career.cornell.edu/resources/surveys/postgraduate.cfm

Life Doesn't Work That Way

Tom Gilovich, the Irene Blecker Rosenfeld Professor of Psychology, College of Arts and Sciences

"Knowing that the most common arcs of success are long and fortuitous can be therapeutic."

Tom Gilovich

As high school was coming to an end, most Cornell students were told by their guidance counselors, their class valedictorians, or their relatives that they should "pursue their passion" or "follow their dreams" in college and beyond. They will hear that advice many times here at Cornell as well. It's good advice, provided that the student has a passion or a reasonably precise dream. But many students, perhaps most, do not. What does the "pursue your passion" mantra do to them?

It makes many students feel deficient. It implies that having a passion, one that translates into a viable career, is the norm. Rather than simply being envious of those students lucky enough to have a burning passion or a clear dream, this frequent refrain can make students feel like they're on the wrong track and that their chances for occupational success and personal well-being are substandard. Rather than inspiring or reassuring students, the phrase feeds many students' already-acute anxieties about life after Cornell.

It also ignores the reality that passion often emerges out of sustained involvement in an activity that one may not have been passionate about initially. With sustained involvement comes skill development, which fosters a sense of mastery that is itself intrinsically rewarding. Those newfound skills, furthermore, make it more likely that a person will be promoted to occupational niches with more autonomy; and engaging in autonomous, effective action is a tremendous boost to well being.

The "pursue your passion" mantra also short-changes the role of chance in people's lives, even the lives of highly successful people. When advisees come to my office and show signs of being anxious about their future trajectory, I encourage them to read biographies. When they do so, they find that it is a rare person who knew in college exactly what he or she wanted to do in life. Biographies are only written about notable individuals, of course, and so my advisees also learn that it is rarer still for people to become notable for something they were determined to do even when they were in college. The more common route is for someone to pursue one path for awhile (with or without great passion), switch to something else, seize an opportunity or connection that appeared out of nowhere, and, voilà, stumble onto the success that inspired his or her biographer. Knowing that the most common arcs of success are long and fortuitous can therefore be therapeutic. My advisees tell me that it makes them feel better about joining the adult world beyond Cornell. (Interpretive caution: Cornell students are polite, and they would be unlikely to tell me that my suggestion to read biographies was a waste of time.)

Must Love Cats. Third-year veterinary student, Kamilla Shmakalova, DVM '14, links her interest in shelter medicine to her memories of stray animals in Russia

The realization of how rare it is to have a deep and clear professional passion at the age of 20 also positions students to take advantage of Cornell's greatest strength. With a university motto of ". . . any person can find instruction in any study," Cornell has a special obligation to offer a vast collection of divergent courses. And it does. Cornell administration and faculty encourage students to sample broadly from the university's diverse curriculum—but that encouragement often falls on the deaf ears of students who believe that they should know now what they want to do for the rest of their lives and that they must do everything they can during their four years here in the service of that passion.

Knowing how often the path to success is circuitous can liberate students to get off a narrow curricular path and sample more broadly from the curriculum. In so doing, they'll meet compelling classmates they would never have met otherwise, they'll open themselves to inspiration from faculty they would never have encountered, and they'll be inspired by subjects they didn't imagine could be so engaging. And, who knows, they just might stumble on their life-long passion.

FOR MORE INFORMATION
Cornell University: cornell.edu
Courses of Study: courses.cornell.edu

Mark Bittman, celebrated *New York Times* food columnist and best-selling cookbook author, cooks with students at Bethe House on West Campus

"Passion often emerges out of sustained involvement in an activity that one may not have been passionate about initially."

Building Our Communities Means Loving Ourselves First

Khamila Alebiosu '13

Khamila Alebiosu '13

"I realized that before I tried to build 'community' on campus, I had to build me. I had to become my biggest fan and number-one supporter."

Cornell taught me how to love myself. Or rather, it forced me to. At a tough place like this, I knew I wasn't going to be able to survive unless I took care of myself. The idea of "self" became important.

On this campus, community is a privilege. As an institution, Cornell can be a confined place rather than an open, fluid space. It does not ask you how you are doing. It will not hold your hand. It will not pay your rent. It will not take those prelims for you. So, at a top Ivy League university that pushes students, we need community. It's something you have to build yourself.

That process varies among all of us. If you're lucky, you find it your first semester. Some find it through their fraternity or sorority, a theatre ensemble, an a cappella group, or a program house. But it takes others some time; hence, the search for community can lead people into unhealthy places. At the bottom of a liquor bottle. In a sexual affair. In conflict with others. I've seen too many Cornellians, including myself, trying to escape in order to be found.

I realized that before I tried to build "community" on campus, I had to build me. I had to become my biggest fan and number-one

Ordinary People, a theater troupe made up of Cornell students dedicated to raising awareness about issues of oppression, performs at the 2012 *Tapestry of Possibilities* theatrical presentation that was followed by an interactive, moderated discussion about diversity

supporter. Since I was away from home, family couldn't be my only support system. I had to be my own. Cornell requires strength, resilience, and self-love.

So, what do you have to do at Cornell? You have to work on you. In May, I left with an Ivy League degree, but my education has surpassed the classroom. I learned how to love myself enough to only want the best—to strive for excellence in my academics, to demand justice for

Members of the student theater troupe Ordinary People perform skits and engage in dialogue with South African students from University of the Free State

myself, to be confident that my passion and determination will take me to great places.

I want my university to be its very best. Over the last four years, I've worked to establish not only community but also justice on campus. I've help create a culture in which students become alumni who care about the Intercultural Center, peer education organizations, and diversity initiatives. I've been part of a campus that recognizes to be worldly, one must acknowledge that other worlds exist and that there is still work to do.

I realize now that community isn't something defined in words but in action. It's building relationships and building bridges. It is collective leadership and working together, not separately. It's where you find compassion, support, love, and motivation. And the word itself, community, includes another key word: "unity." It is important that we continue to strive for unity and solidarity on this campus.

To the new student: community requires *you*. You have to be in it and a part of it. It's opening the door when you see someone carrying a bunch of stuff. It's going to your friend's dance performance. It's standing up for someone and doing what's right. It's being open, aware, and sensitive. It's stopping yourself from saying "that's so retarded" or "that's so gay" or making a rape joke . . . because

community means protecting the space. Owning the space. Respecting the space. Because community requires justice, leadership, and awareness, I took the prerequisite steps to build myself. To become someone who seeks to collaborate, listen, and care.

At Cornell, I learned who I was and what I want and what my purpose is. I stood fighting for justice on the campus because I see it as part of my civic duty and because I owned my role on the campus and wanted the best from it. I learned to love myself enough, to speak up, and to challenge.

Cornell is a tough place, but it makes you tougher. It molds you into someone who stands for something, who gets back up, and who keeps pushing. I want to keep moving forward and take Cornell with me.

I mean, my degree has to live up to my greatness, right?

"I learned how to love myself enough to only want the best—to strive for excellence in my academics, to demand justice for myself, to be confident that my passion and determination will take me to great places."

Cornell Career Services

Rebecca Sparrow, director, Cornell Career Services

Rebecca Sparrow

"Our goal in Cornell Career Services is to help students apply their education and experiences toward advancing their career goals over a lifetime."

Parents and others often ask students—again and again!—"What are you going to do when you graduate?" Some students enter Cornell fairly confident of their answers and stick to their goals. Others have an idea of something they may want to do with their Cornell degree. Still others really do not yet have much of an idea of career goals and may take far longer to decide what they want to do in the future. So you might hear a response from your son or daughter ranging from "I'm going to be a computer programmer," to "I think I want to be a doctor," to "I'm just really not sure."

The truth is that most students are not aware of all their work and career options at the time they enter college. (How many students knew at age 17 or 18 that they might graduate to become a scale management associate or a wheel associate, as members of Cornell's Class of 2012 did?) Another truth is that a student's degree does not have to dictate what career that student will enter. For instance, while a licensed engineer must have studied engineering, a student who studies engineering does not have to become a licensed engineer. That engineering graduate may in fact embark on any of a number of career paths, such as sales, consulting, or financial services.

So, many different answers to the "big career question" are okay. It's also healthy for students to change their minds about their career choices as they continue their academic pursuits and learn more about themselves and what's available in the world of work. The important thing is for students to create a foundation at Cornell upon which to build their professional lives following graduation.

Our goal in Cornell Career Services is to help students apply their education and experiences toward advancing their career goals over a lifetime. Through our various offices in the colleges and in the university-sponsored services in Barnes Hall, our approach is to work with students to *understand* themselves, *explore* their options, and *take action* to pursue their preferred path. Our services are aligned with these three components of our career-development model. We help students identify their interests, values, and strengths and articulate them confidently in resumes, cover letters, interviews, and personal statements. We offer opportunities for students to learn about different career fields through job shadowing, networking events with alumni and others on and off campus, internships, co-ops, and more.

The 2013 Career Fair

Abhiram Varadarajan interviews with Deepak Chokkadi of Everyday Health during the NYC Tech Talent Draft in Sage atrium

Students talk with representatives of Tumblr during the first annual Cornell Career Startup Fair in Duffield Hall

Surgeons mentor pre-med students during rotations at Weill Cornell Medical College

The 2012 Arts and Sciences Career Connections Reception, where students meet alumni with similar academic backgrounds and learn how they applied their education in liberal arts to the world of work

The 2012 Career Day at the School of Hotel Administration

And, we help them implement an effective strategy to attain their desired career outcomes, whether that means applying to graduate, law, or medical school; developing a job-search plan; trying for a prestigious fellowship or award; or exploring opportunities for a "gap-year" or "bridge" experience.

The great thing about learning and applying the career-development model is that it is useful for managing a career over the course of a person's work life. Very few careers follow a linear path; instead they involve multiple steps, including changes in direction from time to time. At every point of change in this zig-zag approach to career management, the steps of understanding, exploring, and taking action are essential for reinforcing overall forward movement.

Across Cornell Career Services, we pride ourselves in offering individualized service to our students, and we welcome them to begin working with us as early as they are ready. In addition to one-on-one advising, we offer a wide array of workshops and programs, job postings, career fairs, mock interviews, on-campus interviews, a career library, a media repository of past events and programs, and technology-driven tools such as Optimal Resume and Optimal Interview. Our calendar of events is on our website— career.cornell.edu—where we also provide extensive information about all the services we offer to students.

We encourage parents and other family members to explore our website to learn what's available. Often you are the ones who can motivate students to take the first step by coming in to see us. We are eager to support your students as they prepare—through their studies, work experiences, and activities—to launch their careers after Cornell.

FOR MORE INFORMATION
Cornell Career Services; career.cornell.edu

"Across Cornell Career Services, we pride ourselves in offering individualized service to our students, and we welcome them to begin working with us as early as they are ready."

The Passion of Cornellians

Charles D. Phlegar, vice president, Division of Alumni Affairs and Development

Charles Phlegar

"Your son or daughter is going to have an amazing four years of personal transformation and growth here."

I have been privileged to work in higher education for more than 30 years and have witnessed many wonderful examples of commitment and loyalty to a particular university or college. But during the course of my career I have rarely, if ever, seen anything like the passion, the excitement, and the commitment that Cornellians have for their alma mater.

Why is that? Ask any Cornell alumnus or alumna, and you will get a broad range of answers. In my opinion, it's a combination of the beauty of this place, its isolation amid the natural splendor of the Finger Lakes, the ups and downs of the weather, and the type of student that chooses to attend Cornell.

Amidst the diversity of Cornell's student body there is a powerful commonality, a humble and strong work ethic. Most of our students aren't wealthy, and many come from families that could not afford to send them to Cornell without extensive financial aid. (Did you know that the number of Cornell undergraduates who receive financial aid exceeds the total undergraduate populations of Ivy League peers such as Harvard, Princeton, or Yale?)

Most of our students come from the heart of this country, its middle class. The achievements of Cornell alumni demonstrate how a college education remains the strongest engine of upward social mobility in this country.

What also makes Cornell so special are the characteristics our students share with our exemplary faculty and staff: concern for each other, compassion for the less fortunate, and their love for this country and their community. It may sound clichéd, but it's true.

You can see those characteristics at work every day at Cornell. Through 30 student-run projects affiliated with Cornell's Public Service Center, more than 7,000 students devote hundreds of thousands of hours to community service each year. Cornell's Greek-letter community, working through the Interfraternity Council, the Multicultural Greek Letter Council, and the Pan-Hellenic Advisory Council, also provide tens of thousands of hours of service to the local community. Many of Cornell's student athletes volunteer to read to children in Ithaca's public schools, and Cornell staff members are active in school boards, town councils, and religious and community organizations throughout the Finger Lakes region.

This ethos of public service was displayed in the fall of 2011, when more than 1,000 Cornell students banded together to coordinate

Left: The 2013 Cornell Alumni Leadership Conference: Working with Students to Effect Change on Campus

volunteer efforts to assist the residents of Owego, New York, who suffered extensive flood damage because of Tropical Storm Irene.

These values of selflessness and mutual support are also on display through the efforts of the 15,000 Cornell alumni who share their expertise and time in some structured way with the university. Working in conjunction with one of the finest alumni affairs and development organizations in the nation, Cornell alumni help advance their alma mater through more than 450 recognized volunteer organizations throughout the world. These organizations hold more than 1,400 events annually and help Cornellians stay engaged with the university's progress. There are thriving hubs of alumni activity in places like New York City, Silicon Valley, Washington, D.C.— and we have a rapidly growing international alumni network. A new Cornell student's decision to attend the university may well have been influenced by the Cornell Alumni Admissions Ambassador Network, whose 9,000 members make it the university's largest alumni volunteer organization.

I'm also the proud parent of a Cornell student, and through the experiences of my daughter, Casey, I've gained a new perspective on the impact that alumni volunteers have on Cornell. Without alumni volunteers, events like Reunion and Homecoming would be much more difficult to stage and much less enjoyable for the university community. Casey, a student in the College of Human Ecology, volunteered as a clerk for Reunion Weekend for the first time after her first year. After she saw how hard alumni volunteers worked to

make Reunion successful, she said, "I can't believe all these people do all this and don't get paid. Why do they do it?"

They do it because they love Cornell and want to see their alma mater give others the opportunities it has afforded them. Your first-year student will one day graduate into a worldwide alumni network that will be of great value if he or she embraces it. And students don't need to wait until after graduation to connect with that network. Students can volunteer to support Reunion and Homecoming, help raise funds through the annual phonathon or the senior class giving program, or support other activities with their time and talent.

By volunteering, our students forge a connection to Cornell that will be with them for the rest of their lives. You may not see it right away, but over time your student's Cornell experiences, especially those after graduation, will be linked to whatever she or he accomplishes in life.

Your son or daughter is going to have an amazing four years of personal transformation and growth here. Encourage your Cornellian to seek out and find ways to contribute through community service or by volunteering on behalf of Cornell. And know that when your student graduates into this great community of alumni, he or she will be positioned to take advantage of all it has to offer.

FOR MORE INFORMATION
Cornell University Alumni: alumni.cornell.edu
Public Service Center: psc.cornell.edu

The Phlegar family: Karen, Lauren, Casey, Kamryn, and Charles

Students provided assistance to flood victims in the communities of Owego and Apalachin after the devastating floods in New York's Southern Tier region in 2011

Students in the Pre-Orientation Service Trips (POST) program help to build a new labyrinth at the Ithaca Children's Garden

"Your first-year student will one day graduate into a worldwide alumni network that will be of great value if he or she embraces it."

Top (left to right): The 2012 Alumni Baseball Game at Reunion / Cornelliana Night at Reunion 2012 / Alumni prepare for the Reunion Row during Reunion 2007 / Alumni enjoy dancing in the Arts Quad tents during Reunion 2009 / Alumni canoeing on Beebe Lake during Reunion 2012 / Laurie Robinson and Bill Nye enjoy dancing in the Arts Quad tents during Reunion 2012 / The 2011 Cornell Alumni Leadership Conference in Washington, D.C.

CORNELL
I YELL
CORNELL!
WORDS BY
T·R·COX·'11
MUSIC BY
H·F·WELCH·'10
5
COPYRIGHT 1909 BY CORNELL
GLEE·BANJO·and MANDOLIN CLUBS
WHEELAN
-'11-

Four Generations of Cornellians

Jeff Weiss '79, managing director, Distributed Sun

Jeff Weiss '79

"Our family's experience demonstrates that
your Cornell narrative will be what you make of it."

Bertrand Weiss, Class of 1909

Welcome to the Cornell family. I hope your family's experience will become as enriching and long standing as mine, which began with my grandfather. He arrived in the fall of 1905, traveling from Omaha, Nebraska. Bertrand Weiss moved to Brooklyn after graduating as a civil engineer and enjoying fraternity life. There he built his engineering business in consulting on the construction of office and public buildings, including post offices and dams. He raised a family in New Rochelle, New York, from which my father Donald joined the Cornell Class of 1949 and graduated as a mechanical engineer. Dad was also a cheerleader, which we now imagine is why his dad, Bert Weiss, penned the alumni verse to the "Song of the Classes" on the occasion of Don's graduation.

Turning to this century, after growing up in Washington, D.C., my son, Peter, graduated in 2011 and my daughter, Catherine, is in the Class of 2014. My niece, Amanda, arrived at what she calls "the family school" from Lincolnshire, Illinois, and is a member of the Class of 2015. I extend my warmest welcome as president of the Class of 1979.

Cornell's dazzling array of opportunities will help your student write his or her score. While this will include academic studies and a choice of major, your student's manuscript will be highlighted by friendships, clubs, roommates, and living choices and will be punctuated by memories, contributions, and achievements. As you hug your son or daughter before leaving campus, know this is a time he or she will make his or her own way, take risks, set goals, and stretch personal boundaries!

I first arrived at Cornell from Highland Park, Illinois, in 1974. Then a high school junior, I attended the Cornell summer school program. I lived at Clara Dickson Hall and took classes in international law and economics 101. The international law class included a captain from the Israeli Army who had a lot of then-current experience to guide the class discussion. Glorious weather and scores of new friends forged an exceptional summer. Returning home, I applied for early decisions to the School of Arts and Sciences, convinced it would be the perfect home for me.

Week one in North Campus Six offered a number of "firsts," such as having a roommate, mine from Delaware, and living in a co-ed dorm. How agreeable! Amazingly, half of the class officers of the Class of 1979 more than 30 years later, were in that dorm freshman year and two attended the high school summer session with me. So, as students enter their dorm and make friends, they should know that the next person they meet might truly become a friend for life.

Professor LaFeber, 1970

Two memories remain vibrant from my first few days. The first involves the freshman writing seminar requirement that was much the same then as it is now. Researching options, I discovered that a Cornell professor whose work I had read was teaching; however, Walter LaFeber required an interview. Little did I know then that our first meeting would lead to my majoring in U.S. foreign policy and that I would enroll in Professor LaFeber's courses for six semesters.

My second discovery that first week was that all the guys I met seemed to have been invited to do something I had not. It took some inquiry to understand that the rowing coach had sent invitations to row to all entering males who stood taller than five

feet, ten inches and to cox to those less than five feet, seven inches. The few of us with statures in between received no letter.

I became the first liberal arts Cornellian from my family, following two engineers. I loved the analysis and debate required for U.S. foreign policy and coupled it with economics to begin a business curriculum.

In addition to my double major in history and economics, I wanted to take general business classes, such as accounting and statistics. These were available in other Cornell colleges, and I took many of them. Apparently I was among the first to form a business minor by combining classes from various schools, and I helped to author the first Cornell Management Guide.

Let me encourage exploration in new areas of study possibly outside one's comfort zone. Entering my senior year, I realized I had yet to take a class in the English department, and I wanted to. I selected a senior seminar. I reasoned that since my favorite classes in my majors were seminars, the same would be true in English. This particular course, Nineteenth-Century English Poetry, was designed for English majors and taught by a visiting professor from Oxford. In the first weeks of the class, I discovered I was lost. While I knew the literal meaning of all the individual words I read, I simply could not discern the inferred meaning these English majors elicited. I struggled, and when it came time to write a term paper, I chose William Blake's "Marriage of Heaven and Hell." The reason was that the text is illustrated. I hoped

Left: Jeff, Christie, and Peter Weiss at NCAA wrestling

Above and right: Catherine and Jeff Weiss at Cornell

Above: Don Weiss
Right: Peter and Jeff Weiss on a Bosphorus cruise

Left: Amanda, Catherine, and Jeff Weiss at a Cornell dinner

that perhaps the cartoons would help my understanding. When the professor graded that essay she commented that I was the first person to her knowledge to assess the economic and class implications from this text. All poets and English majors know that the text is a treatise on religion. I missed that meaning, but formulated an entirely new perspective. I adored the class.

My son Peter graduated from the School of Hotel Administration with a concentration in real estate. Catherine is a neuropsychology major and Latin American studies minor, while my niece, Amanda, majors in nutrition science. The university's motto states that "any person can find instruction in any study" —our family is a testament.

We also enjoyed fraternity and sorority life. My grandfather joined a fraternity in 1906, now gone from campus, which was one of the first at Cornell to admit members of multiple religious faiths. Dad joined Pi Lambda Phi in 1946 and maintained friendships with fraternity brothers his entire life. I joined Alpha Delta Phi in 1976, lived in the house for three years, and retain many

active friendships with brothers. Peter joined Chi Psi. Catherine is a Kappa Kappa Gamma. Amanda joined Alpha Chi Omega. While we all joined different houses, each enjoyed and benefited from the ties of a small group bonded together with social, literary, and living camaraderie.

Truly, Cornell is a place your student can find his or her way and where all students will make their home. My family story is only one example of how Cornell helps people of varied interests, personalities, and professional ambitions excel. Our family's experience demonstrates that your Cornell narrative will be what you make of it. To the neophyte students I say: When you arrive, be curious. Take initiative. Meet people: faculty and coaches. Explore. Challenge yourself to really get to know new friends. You have achieved so much already, which is why Cornell offered you an admissions invitation. You have taken the first step by accepting that offer. Now find ways to reach beyond your personal boundaries. Anything you aspire to accomplish can be achieved on your new campus. It is up to you to make it so!

> "The university's motto states that 'any person can find instruction in any study'— our family is a testament."

Above and directly above: Members of the Weiss family at Peter's graduation